THE POLITICS OF SOLZHENITSYN

THE POLITICS OF SOLZHENITSYN

STEPHEN CARTER
Senior Lecturer in Politics and Government
City of London Polytechnic

HOLMES & MEIER PUBLISHERS, INC.
New York

891. 78

SoLZHENITSYN

First published in the United States of America 1977 by
HOLMES & MEIER PUBLISHERS, INC
101 Fifth Avenue
New York, N.Y. 10003

Printed in Great Britain

905473

Library of Congress Cataloging in Publication Data

Carter, Stephen.
  The politics of Solzhenitsyn.

  Bibliography: p.
  Includes index.
  1. Solzhenitsyn, Aleksandr Isaevich, 1918– —Political and social
views. I. Title. PG3488.04Z595   891.7'8'4409   76–28346

ISBN 0–8419–0244–5

In memory of past sufferings, this book is
dedicated to Russia's future in a peaceful world

Contents

Acknowledgements

The author and publishers wish to thank the following who have kindly given permission for the use of copyright material from Alexander Solzhenitsyn's publications.

Nicholas Bethell for extracts from the English translation of Solzhenitsyn's *Nobel Prize Lecture*. Reprinted by permission also of the copyright holders of the Russian text, *The Nobel Foundation*, © 1972.

The Bodley Head and Farrar, Straus & Giroux, Inc., for extracts from :
Stories and Prose Poems, (Dlia pol'zy Dela) translated by Michael Glenny. Translation copyright © 1970, 1971 Michael Glenny. World copyright © 1970 Alexander Solzhenitsyn. Published in Germany under the title Im Interesse der Sache, by Luchterhand Verlag, copyright © 1970 by Hermann Luchterhand Verlag, GmbH, Neuwied und West Berlin;

Cancer Ward, translated by Nicholas Bethell and David Burg. Translation © 1968, 1969 The Bodley Head. Russian copyright © 1968 Alexander Solzhenitsyn; *August 1914* (Augoust Tchetyrnadtsatoguo), translated by Michael Glenny. Translation copyright © 1972 Michael Glenny. Russian text first published by YMCA-Press, Paris. World copyright © 1971 Alexander Solzhenitsyn; *The Love-Girl and the Innocent*, translated by Nicholas Bethell and David Burg. Translation copyright © 1969 The Bodley Head. Copyright © 1969 Alexander Solzhenitsyn.

Wm Collins Sons & Company Limited and Harper & Row Publishers Inc. for extracts from *The First Circle* and *The Gulag Archipelago*, Volumes I and II.

Wm Collins Sons & Company Limited and Little, Brown & Company for extracts from *From Under the Rubble* by Alexander Solzhenitsyn, Mikhail Agursky, A B Evgeny Barbanov, Vadim Borisov, F. Korsakof, and Igor Shafarevich. Copyright © 1974 by YMCA-Press, Paris.

Victor Gollancz Limited and E. P. Dutton & Company Inc. for extracts from *One Day in the Life of Ivan Denisovich*. English translation copyright © 1963. Reprinted by permission of the publishers.

Penguin Books Limited and Harper & Row Inc. for extracts from *Solzhenitsyn—A Documentary Record* edited by Leopold Labedz (Allen Lane, 1970) © Leopold Labedz 1970.

Writers and Scholars International Limited, London, for extracts from the *Letter to Soviet Leaders*.

Preface

My main reason for writing this book is simple: Aleksandr Solzhenitsyn is saying something which is important, not only for Russia and the USSR but also for us in the West. At the same time he has been very widely misunderstood and misrepresented, particularly by political scientists. It is always unwise, and often dangerous, to misunderstand those who are saying something important.

In writing this book, I have been aware of Solzhenitsyn's bitter protest to the editorial board of *Literaturnaya Gazeta* in which he stated: 'I know your paper will not publish a single line of mine without attributing to it a distorted, erroneous meaning.'* I have made efforts to avoid bias and distortion, in so far as this is humanly possible. I have therefore concentrated on a textual analysis, giving quotations from Solzhenitsyn's prose works to substantiate my general conclusions. Since a great deal of Solzhenitsyn's work has been hurriedly, poorly and insensitively translated into English, often without adequate consultation with the author, I have checked most of the extracts quoted with the equivalent passages in Russian, using (largely) texts in English which are listed in the bibliography. I have not been as thorough in this field as I should have been, and the seasoned eye will see from my notes at the end of each chapter where my work could be improved. But I have tried to serve the truth, and therefore, despite patchy scholarship, I believe the true outlines have emerged.

This raises the question of the accuracy and authenticity of the Russian texts. I am aware that many 'pirate' editions of Solzhenitsyn's works exist. I decided to work from the six-volume *Sobranie Sochinenii* of Solzhenitsyn, published by Possev (Frankfurt), and for later works, I relied on the YMCA press in Paris (*Gulag Archipelago*, Parts I–VII, *The Calf and the Oak, Lenin in Zürich* and *From Under the Rubble*). Some important primary sources were contained in the *Herald of the Russian Christian Movement* and in *Continent*, among which were some of the missing chapters from *The First Circle*. I worked on *August 1914* from an edition published in 1971 by Flegon Press, but I regret to say that this is a pirated version. I have not been able to obtain the screen play *The Tanks Know the Truth*, nor *The Feast of the Victors*, but this last has in any

* *Russkaya Mysl'* (22 May 1969).

case been repudiated by the author. Finally, we have yet to see *Decembrists without December*, *The Republic of Labour*, *October 1916*, *March 1917*, and *April 1917* if this is complete.

However, I feel justified in writing this book now because it seems to me that there is some considerable demand for clarification. In order to help the reader through, I have provided summaries at the end of each chapter: this will aid those who are less than familiar with Solzhenitsyn's works or the names of his characters.

I realise that there is a problem of *attribution* in much of the literary analysis. For example, are the ideas expressed by Varsonifiev in *August 1914* those of Solzhenitsyn? Does Kostoglotov in *Cancer Ward* exactly mirror the author's views at that time? And what are we to say of such characters as Shulubin in *Cancer Ward*, who advocates a philosophy of 'ethical socialism'? I have tried to solve this problem by attempting to locate themes which are in some sense pervasive; and I trust that the reader will allow me to rely on occasions on plausibility and the application of commonsense. Nevertheless, I quote the required passages in the text so that the reader may judge for himself or herself.

My thanks are due to Professor L. B. Schapiro, Ellen de Kadt and Peter Reddaway of the London School of Economics and Political Science, and to John B. Dunlop of Oberlin College, who read some of my chapters and made valuable critical comments. However, I take personal responsibility for all the opinions expressed here, and for any errors. I would like to thank Xenia Howard-Johnston for her tolerant custodianship of the Russian Reading Room at the LSE, and her helpful attitude which persisted even at late times on Fridays. My thanks go to my former fellow students Linda Aldwinkle and Joe Winogradoff for their invaluable help in translation and criticism. I gratefully acknowledge the encouraging attitude taken towards me this academic year at the City of London Polytechnic, Unit of Political Studies, and in particular I am grateful to Mrs Renée Gerson for releasing me temporarily from my administrative duties, and to Dr René Saran for carrying out those duties in my mental and often physical absences. The patience, accuracy and sheer hard work of Mrs Lynda Andaloussi and Mrs Elizabeth Ellis in producing the typescript to time deserve the highest praise. I would like to thank the Macmillan Press for their help in producing this work in the United Kingdom and Holmes & Meier for their contribution in the United States. Last, but not least, I acknowledge my debt to a tolerant and supportive wife and family.

S. K. C.

1 Aleksandr Solzhenitsyn as a Political Writer

What are the politics of Solzhenitsyn? By this I mean, what are his political views? What significance do these views have for us in the West, or for the Soviet Union? These are important questions, since Solzhenitsyn is no longer merely a great Russian writer but also a man who has had some considerable influence on public opinion, legislatures and governments. And yet few understand his proposals as a coherent whole and the political content of these proposals often seems obscure. Solzhenitsyn himself is reluctant to make explicit the nature of his political programme: indeed, he has frequently denied that he is a political figure at all. He has stated that

> it is not the task of the writer to defend or criticise . . . one or another mode of government organisation. The task of the writer is to select more universal and eternal questions [such as] the secrets of the human heart and conscience, the confrontation between life and death, the triumph over spiritual sorrow, the laws in the history of mankind.[1]

In June 1967 he was questioned by Soviet officials about the appearance of *Cancer Ward* in the West, and about his open letter to the Fourth Soviet Writers' Congress. In answer to the charge made by G. Markov that the open letter, although legal, was unprecedented, an attempt to form a 'fraction', and at the least a dishonest kind of politics, Solzhenitsyn replied, 'What politics? I am only an artist.'[2]

It is important ro realise that Solzhenitsyn believes his message to be primarily moral, aesthetic and religious, rather than political. He repeatedly criticises politics and politicians. He believes that political programmes are likely to be untrustworthy, less than the truth. In this he resembles the Russian philosopher N. Berdyayev who made a distinction between the (relative) truth of the political intelligentsia, and the (absolute) truth of philosophy.[3] But it would be absurd to say that Solzhenitsyn has *no* political proposals and no political influence. How then are we to resolve this paradox? What do these political proposals amount to?

In answer to the first question, it seems to me that we must try to see the work of Solzhenitsyn in its correct, Russian context, and not from a Western point of view. In the Russian tradition, the open clash and conflict of political views (which are typical of a parliamentary democracy) have been extremely uncommon historically. In a totalitarian state, any form of opposition politics is dangerous, and under Stalin it was mortally dangerous. Within the traditions of the Communist Party of the Soviet Union since at least 1921, any form of 'fractionalism' has been banned. However, another Russian tradition, the moral and political role of the writer, acts as a countervailing force to these tendencies. As Solzhenitsyn's character Innokenti Volodin says in *The First Circle*, 'Aren't writers supposed to teach, to guide? . . . And for a country to have a great writer . . . is like having another government.'[4] Thus it is that in Russia, a non-political figure, a writer or an artist, may have profound political influence. Finally, some important traditions of Russian political thought, Slavophilism of the 1840s, the 'Native Soil Movement' of the 1860s, and N. A. Berdayayev in the early decades of the twentieth century, have sought to replace politics with a moral or religious approach, and it seems to me that Solzhenitsyn has some affinity with these intellectual trends, and has been influenced to some extent by them.

I hope to elucidate the content of Solzhenitsyn's political thought in two stages. Part One is a largely literary, textual analysis including a discussion of the *Gulag Archipelago*. Part Two is a textual analysis based on Solzhenitsyn's more recent, more directly political works and speeches.

Aleksandr Isaevich Solzhenitsyn was born on 11 December 1918 at Kislovodsk in the Caucasus. He is thus a 'child of the revolution', having lived all his life under Lenin and his heirs. As Kostoglotov in *Cancer Ward* says, 'I'll always be younger than this society. What do you expect me to do, keep silent all my life?'[5] Solzhenitsyn was a mere boy as Stalin rose to power, and his talents in the fields of mathematics, physics and literature began to develop as the Great Purges of 1934–8 reached their climax. Unable to pursue his talents beyond graduation at Rostov University and at the Moscow Institute of Philosophy, Literature and History (a course completed by correspondence), on account of the call-up for army service, Solzhenitsyn served his country in a war in which strategy was often most ineptly conducted, over the heads of his generals, by Stalin. Solzhenitsyn, the hardened soldier twice decorated for gallantry as an artillery officer, was 'rewarded' with incarceration in a series of prisons, because of minor criticism of Stalin in a private letter to a friend.

Solzhenitsyn's talents were useful to the state in so far as his knowledge of physics and electronics could be used. Sometimes these talents were called upon by the security organs for the surveillance of private conversations and telephone calls, in the special prison near Moscow (called 'Mavrino' in *The First Circle*). But when Solzhenitsyn's ability had been utilised to some extent, and he refused further cooperation, he was transferred to the Karlag concentration camp in Dzezkazgan (Karaganda), which perhaps provided some of the background for *One Day in the Life of Ivan Denisovich*. Solzhenitsyn managed to survive here, finding happiness not only in his literary compositions but also in such simple tasks as building a wall, or in simple comforts such as an extra bowl of skilly and a little tobacco (like Ivan Denisovich Shukhov). And at the end of *One Day* in such a camp, Shukhov was able to say, 'Glory be to Thee, O Lord.'[6] By contrast Stalin's days and nights are represented in *The First Circle* as a twilight world of isolation, paranoia and imagined plots, perhaps on the borders of madness.[7]

On Stalin's death, Solzhenitsyn too was incurably ill. He was banished to exile 'in perpetuity' near Dzambul in southern Kazakhstan, but recovered miraculously after treatment for cancer in Tashkent. With the change of atmosphere after Stalin's death, Solzhenitsyn was released from exile and rehabilitated in 1956. On moving to Riazan, he was eventually joined by his (first) wife Reshetovskaya.

Khrushchev's consolidation of power, and the process of de-Stalinisation which led hesitantly to the removal of Stalin's body from the Red Square mausoleum after the XXII Congress, saw Solzhenitsyn's abrupt rise to fame after the publication of *One Day in the Life of Ivan Denisovich* in November 1962. However, after this, only a few more of Solzhenitsyn's works appeared officially in the Soviet Union, including *Matryona's Home* and *For the Good of the Cause*, in Tvardovskii's literary magazine *Novyi Mir*. Solzhenitsyn's personal account of this period, *The Oak and the Calf*, clarifies much about his literary fortunes, his tactics and strategy, the conditions under which he and his friends worked. More than this, *The Oak and the Calf* tells us of a political evolution which may prove instructive to others opposing the authorities in the USSR.

After the appearance of *One Day in the Life of Ivan Denisovich*, Solzhenitsyn compared himself to some kind of 'deep water fish' which did not know what to do after it had found itself suddenly at the surface, exposed to public view.[8] What, then, was this fish doing in its lower depths? Earlier, Solzhenitsyn referred to his 'literary conspiracy', his 'cunning threads',[9] showing a dedication of an unusual kind over a long period of time to a definite aim. For many years in the 1960s commentators both West and East tried to depict Solzhenitsyn as a socialist-realist writer, such as Georgi Lukács,[10] while others seized on the phrase of Shulubin in *Cancer Ward* which referred to 'ethical socialism'. Robin Blackburn dismissed Solzhenitsyn as a populist, a plebeian–peasant writer,[11] and some Western communists approved of him because he had been sanctioned by Khrushchev and the XXII Congress of the

CPSU. However, after the appearance of *August 1914* and the *Letter to Soviet Leaders* in the 1970s, a chorus of equally erroneous but this time hostile analysis emerged in particular from left-wing commentators, such as Alan Myers.[12] In fact Solzhenitsyn's aims and beliefs have exhibited a consistency and purpose, over a period of decades, which has only been matched in modern times by Lenin.

It is true that in his incriminating letter of 1945 to his friend Vitkevich, Solzhenitsyn spoke of the 'correctness of Marxism–Leninism'. It need hardly be argued today that Solzhenitsyn is strongly opposed to Marxism–Leninism, but the evolution of his thoughts from 1945 remains obscure in some respects. Perhaps one crucial episode was his conversion, or reconversion, to Christianity, which took place some time in his camp and exile years. Many concurrent influences must have been present, but the episode of one B. N. Kornfeld's influence on Solzhenitsyn during his recovery from an operation, and Kornfeld's astonishing death, as recorded in *Gulag Archipelago*, Book II (Part 4), seems particularly important.[13]

Solzhenitsyn seems to have been determined to interpret the post-revolutionary experience of Russia as an (instructive) disaster, stemming from Marxism and Lenin, as well as from Stalin. He believes that he has a binding duty to represent all those who were murdered and oppressed by Soviet rule, and to oppose communism everywhere. He says,

> However, I did not have the right to take my personal point of view into account, nor to consider what Novyi Mir would think about me, but instead I had constantly to bear in mind, that my literary destiny was not just my own affair; it was also that of those millions who did not write, whisper, or even gasp out the story of their imprisonment, their last testament from the camps.[14]

He claims that this feeling of duty and of destiny affected him as early as 1945, when after his arrest he had a presentiment that just *because* of this arrest he would be able to influence the fate of his country.[15] Only once since 1945 has this idea become weak, and that was in 1965 after the confiscation of his archive by the KGB on 11 September. He failed at the time to see how he could recover from this blow, and he contemplated suicide for the first and last time in his life.[16] Most characteristically, however, he is positive and hopeful, saying for example that

> familiarity with Russian history might well have long ago killed any wish to discover some hand of justice, some higher cosmic meaning in the story of Russia's sufferings; but during my life, since my years in camp, I had become accustomed to being aware of this guiding hand, this meaning which was full of light, and which did not depend on me.[17]

Even in his darkest days, while he and Sakharov were under heavy attack in late 1973, and Sakharov experienced a deep depression, Solzhenitsyn did not give up hope; 'for my whole life, despite logic, I have never experienced this depression, but on the contrary some kind of absurd belief in victory.'[18]

After his arrest in February 1974, he even believed that it was just possible that he would be taken before the Politburo.[19]

The Oak and the Calf reveals a picture of a determined and self-disciplined man, deeply and almost unshakably convinced of his duty and high purpose, whose strategy was consistent throughout the period dealt with, but whose tactics varied over time. At first, he tried the approach of cautious education of public opinion through limited and selective publication of his literary work, beginning with *One Day in the Life of Ivan Denisovich*. He accepted some revisions to his works, especially from the editorial board of *Novyi Mir* under Aleksandr Trifonovich Tvardovskii, and he planned to publish *The First Circle* in an 87-part version, withholding nine chapters which he thought would not be accepted by the censor. Similarly, he withheld part of *August 1914* relating to Lenin, in the hope that the rest might be published in the USSR. The fall of Khrushchev in October 1964 signalled the start of a new phase. Solzhenitsyn realised that the revelations about Stalin at the XX and XXII Congresses of the party, developments which Khrushchev had set in motion, were being slowed down, even reversed. (Solzhenitsyn remarks that this was inevitable because the revelations had not gone far enough and that Khrushchev, like Tvardovskii, had been held captive by the accepted ideology.) The fall of Khrushchev also released Solzhenitsyn from a debt of honour;[20] now he felt that he owed the establishment nothing.

After the emotional and spiritual nadir of September 1965, and the trial of Sinyavskii and Daniel, he became tougher, more self-reliant and more uncompromising. He remarked at the time of the seizure of his archive that the help of Western opinion could not be relied on: Russians would have ultimately to rely only on themselves.

> If we too are to become free, then we must free ourselves. If the twentieth century has a lesson for mankind, then we will give it to the West, but not the West to us: As a result of too much complacent well-being, the will and the reason (of the Western world) have become weak.[21]

By 1966, he realised that he might as well give talks and interviews, because he felt that what he had done up to that time was insufficient and that he had nothing to lose.[22] In November 1966, Solzhenitsyn read some chapters from *Cancer Ward* in public, and gave a speech at the Lazarevskii Institute of Oriental Studies. He recalls that every comment seemed to go off in the hall like gunpowder, for people there were so desperately in need of truth. 'It seemed, for the first time – for the first time in my life, I felt, I saw, that I was making history.'[23]

Following this new line, in the spring of 1967, he took one of the biggest decisions of his life, namely to protest and carry on his public activities rather than quietly writing his major work on the first revolutionary month of 1917. The immediate result of this decision was the famous Open Letter to the Fourth Soviet Writers' Congress. This gave him a feeling of being on a solid foundation.[24] When later Solzhenitsyn was called upon to explain the widespread 'samizdat' reading of *Cancer Ward* and its appearance in the West, as well as the Open Letter, he and Tvardovskii took a firm stand against the Soviet officials. Tvardovskii attributed the publication of *Cancer Ward* in the West, among other things, to unwarranted delays in publication at home. At the end of the meeting, two of the officials, G. Markov and K. Voronkov, actually thanked Tvardovskii and Solzhenitsyn. Solzhenitsyn remarks:

> On that day for the first time in my life I was aware of what I had formerly understood only obliquely: what it means to display strength. And how well they understood that language! *Only this language!* One language only – from the very day of their birth![25]

Solzhenitsyn compares his subsequent grilling (22 September 1967) before the Secretariat of the Union of Writers, in which he manfully answered all criticisms, to the battle of Borodino.

This new orientation to open opposition did not preclude Solzhenitsyn from working hard at his writing. He found that he had gained the strength to 'write, what three years before seemed mortally dangerous. My direction became all the clearer – to victory or death.'[26] In April 1968, *Cancer Ward* appeared in the West under somewhat mysterious circumstances, apparently through the mediation of a KGB agent. The aim of this tortuous procedure was apparently to implicate Solzhenitsyn as a 'class enemy' according to the Brezhnev thesis put forward at a meeting of Moscow Party activists in March 1968 (crudely put, this doctrine states that those 'slandering' the Soviet Union abroad are class enemies). This hectic period was however followed by a period of relative calm. Solzhenitsyn apparently finished his *Gulag Archipelago* on the very day that his 87-part *First Circle* appeared in the West, in June 1968. He tried immediately to revise the real, 96-part *First Circle*, but 'it fell from my hands, I could not work'. He sought his refreshment in prayer and the June countryside, feeling that his duty before the dead was overwhelming: 'They died and you lived – carry out your duty so that the world shall know *everything*.'[27]

The next crucial phase for Solzhenitsyn was the invasion of Czechoslovakia.[28] It confirmed his undying hostility to the regime and seemed to kill any lingering hopes of reform from within. He says later that polycentrist ideas of Communism seem implausible: It is 'impossible to be communist AND Russian, communist AND French. It is necessary to choose.'[29] His convictions about the nature of the regime did not yet make him more openly hostile, for now he wished to preserve his completed *Gulag Archipelago* for the West, and he calculated that this would be a more damaging blow. Thus at this point he became once again more circumspect, failing to protest openly at the invasion. However, this more cautious approach did not save him in the following year from being expelled from the Writers' Union (12 November 1969). Hence he made what he describes as his first *overtly* political protest (his Open Letter to the Secretariat of the RSFSR Union of Writers). In doing this, he was influenced by the opinion of Lydia Korneevna Chukovskaya, who had said that while the 'arrow' was still embedded, one could do nothing, write nothing important. It was necessary to pull it out.[30] Having written it, he reported that it gave him 'great pleasure, freedom of spirit'.[31] At the same time, he had become convinced that he had to remain within the Soviet Union, not only because Russia (despite persecution) was conducive to his writing, but also because his close friend Alya (Natalya Svetlova) had persuaded him that his works and his influence would not penetrate the 'iron shell' of the USSR so well from abroad. Thus his position in this new phase was a complicated one: he was persecuted by the regime and could no longer hope to publish in the Soviet Union. He in his turn was confirmed and dedicated in his opinions about the regime after the invasion of Czechoslovakia. Yet he wanted to remain in Russia, and to work in secret on his literary conspiracy. He badly needed some outside help, and in 1970 this came in the form of the Nobel Prize for Literature. He says bravely that if that prize had not come in 1970, he 'would have started the battle without it', but he adds, it came, and put to rights 'all the mistakes of 1962, mistakes of sluggishness and concealment'.[32] The Nobel Prize thus confirmed Solzhenitsyn in his existing tactics, but it gave his cause an added boost in the form of massive Western interest and international support. This became especially strong after the Soviet authorities responded to the Prize as though it had been a deliberate political provocation by the West. They indicated quite clearly that if Solzhenitsyn were to leave in order to collect his prize, then he might not be allowed to return. Solzhenitsyn says of this episode,

> In spite of the seeming immovability of our state, the initiative did not pass from my hands: from first to last I behaved as though they (the authorities) did not exist, I ignored them: I myself made the decisions, announced that I would go, and they did not try to dissuade

me, then I myself took the decision that I would not go, and exposed our shameful police-state methods. . . .[33]

Although the Award of the Nobel Prize for Literature strengthened Solzhenitsyn's position, his domestic life at this time was emotionally disturbed. He mentioned that he was ready to go abroad in the winter of 1970 to receive his Nobel Prize, even though this would have coincided with the birth of his first son by Alya (Svetlova), namely Yermolai. There is surprisingly little information in *The Oak and the Calf* about Solzhenitsyn's personal relationships with Reshetovskaya or his second wife Svetlova. This lack of information shows Solzhenitsyn to be a man primarily dedicated to his work, seeing his family ties and personal relationships as quite separate from his literary goals. In early 1971, he says, 'For the last five years I endured a profound abyss of family discord and put aside all attempts at its resolution . . . every time because of a shortage of time for finishing work, or part of a work. . . .'[34] As a result, regular crises ensued. Any future biographer should try sympathetically to understand the effect of Solzhenitsyn's marital strains on his character and his work.

In 1971, he began to concentrate more on his historical studies which begin with *August 1914*. He refers to these as 'knots', crucial concurrencies of events and personalities on which the historian should concentrate his attention. He states that the main aim of his 'knots' has been to expose to our view the real Lenin. Solzhenitsyn had originally planned twenty such knots, which should have taken him 40–50 years to write. However, by the time that Lenin was firmly in control in Petrograd (Solzhenitsyn believes), his contribution to history became clear. Hence the first three knots, and complete research for a fourth, became Solzhenitsyn's immediate aim (*August 1914, October 1916, March 1917* and *April 1917*). He gave himself until spring 1975 to write these. Soon afterwards, he arranged for photocopies of all the 'missing' and unpublished parts of his work to be sent to the West, by the most ingenious means. For example, although his telephone at his country cabin (Rozhdestvo) was sometimes tapped, he would telephone a warmly solicitous 'good-night' to his wife, then leave a night-light burning in his bedroom window: after which he would leave on foot through woods and fields to a distant suburban station, and thence to his contact with the microfilm, returning by a different route to his bed in the small hours. 'Only from this moment [when his works were safely in the West] was I really ready for the battle and for death.'[35]

From now on, his real aims and beliefs became much clearer, especially after his Open Letter to the Patriarch Pimen and the appearance of *August 1914* in the West in 1972. Before this, the public and the censorship had thought that he was protesting only about the abuses of the Stalin period, but in fact he wanted to go deeper and to speak more accurately about the origins of Stalin's rise to power. In just the same way as the fall of Khrushchev had released Solzhenitsyn from his debt of honour to the establishment, it seems to me that the death of Tvardovskii and his funeral (27 December 1971) may have similarly released Solzhenitsyn from his obligation to Tvardovskii, who, as a prominent member of the Party, could hardly be seen to be the patron and friend of one who rejected the Russian revolution.

Now Solzhenitsyn's work in Russia moved into a new phase. His Nobel Prize speech of August 1972 was not well received, nor indeed was it very clearly understood, for reasons which I have suggested below (chapter 10). He tried to keep a low profile, concentrating on his historical works (*October 1916* was almost completed by the summer of 1973). For this reason, he had in the early 1970s failed to protest on behalf of Grigorenko or Bukovskii, and now he failed to speak out on behalf of Maximov, expelled in 1973 from the Union of Writers. But the authorities stepped up their attacks on him, not only openly in the press, but also through means which Solzhenitsyn says are typical of the Soviet system, namely the illegal actions of the KGB. He began to receive anonymous letters from 'gangsters', making all kinds of threats including threats on his life. Moreover his personal affairs had reached a crisis point, in that he was forced, owing to his divorce, to leave his dacha Rozhdestvo (the property was in his wife's name). This further disrupted his work. In August 1973 he took leave of the beloved place. He said that he had always been able to write there:

> However exhausted, shaken up, or distracted I might be when I arrived here, some kind of inspiration would pour into me from the greenery, from the water, the silver birches and willows, from the oaken benches, from the table above the little stream – and after two hours I found I could already write again. It was a miracle. . . .[36]

Despite his sadness, at the end of August Solzhenitsyn moved over again to the attack by giving a press interview to the Associated Press Agency and *Le Monde* on 23 August 1973. At the very same time, *Gulag Archipelago* had been seized in typescript form by the KGB, who had forced Solzhenitsyn's associate Elizabeth Voronyanskaya, after days and nights of interrogation, to reveal its whereabouts. Solzhenitsyn says that although the disaster was far and away more serious than the seizure of 1965, he was still not dismayed. 'But my mood, my sensations, were quite different: I had no sense of doom, of the destruction of life, as I had experienced before, and I even had almost no sense of defeat.'[37]

Attacks in the Soviet press against Sakharov and Solzhenitsyn swelled to a climax in the summer of 1973. Few people in the West will be able to understand the fear that an all-out Soviet press campaign can instill into an ordinary Soviet citizen. In Stalin's day, such attacks meant that the person concerned was already doomed, and the mass of people would know that they were required to howl for his blood. Solzhenitsyn and Sakharov have exhibited courage of a superhuman order. Solzhenitsyn, indeed, simply and calmly worked out what the authorities were likely to do next. He knew that the *Gulag Archipelago* was utterly dangerous and hostile to the Soviet system, a deadly blow. Surely the authorities would try to respond in kind? Solzhenitsyn calculated that the authorities might just conceivably seek to kill him. One possible alternative was that they would try to negotiate, and this is in fact what happened, through the medium of his former wife, Natalya Reshetovskaya, who relayed the offer to publish *Cancer Ward* in the USSR under certain conditions, which included a long period of silence and totally restricted publication. He refused, understanding with sudden horror that his former wife was now an agent of the KGB. In December 1973, Solzhenitsyn had rejected any attempts at negotiation, and he was thus ready for the final battle. 'For the first time, the first time I went out to the battle at my full height and voice.'[38] At that time, Western reaction was very strong and united, as it had not been since the invasion of Czechoslovakia. Solzhenitsyn believed at that time that Russia was at last 'beginning to *wake up*'.[39] (Since then, he has concluded, rather, that it is the West which has been asleep.)

In the New Year, 1974, the Soviet news agency TASS responded to the *Gulag Archipelago*, whose first part had appeared in Paris, with extreme hostility. Solzhenitsyn realised intellectually that all hope of changing opinion from within Russia had ceased, but it seems that emotionally he hoped still that some sudden change was possible. Hence he resolved not to flee immediately but to give his next public appearance from an internal address.[40] Moreover he gave orders to withhold for a time the publication of his *Letter to Soviet Leaders*. However, he was not ready for what did in fact occur in February 1974. He was surprised at his wife's Moscow flat by an overwhelming force of KGB men and, without formal arrest, he was taken to the Lefortovo prison and charged with treason (Article 64 of the 1960 Criminal Code). However, perhaps owing to his courageous stance before the procurator Malyarov, and to the strength of Western reaction, he was sent post-haste in a commandeered civil aircraft to West Germany. He compared himself to the calf which butted the oak tree in Russian legend: 'The oak did not fall. But did it not seem to bend? Did it not yield a bit? And the calf's forehead remained intact. . . .'[41]

Since 1974, Solzhenitsyn has been living in and near Zurich, making visits to Stockholm, the USA, France, Britain, Spain, and other Western countries.

NOTES

1   *Sobranie Sochinenii,* Possev (1970), Vol. 6, p. 53.
2   *Bodalsya telyonok s dubom,* YMCA, Paris (1975), p. 190.
3   N. A. Berdyayev (b. 1874), in *Vekhi,* Moscow (1909).
4   *Sob. Soch.,* Vol. 4, p. 503.
5   *Sob. Soch.,* Vol. 2, pp. 452–3.
6   *Sob. Soch.,* Vol. 1, p. 127.
7   *The First Circle,* Collins/Fontana (1970), chapters 18–21.
8   *Bodalsya telyonok s dubom, op. cit.,* p. 59.
9   *Ibid.,* pp. 42–3.
10 G. Lukács, *Solzhenitsyn,* Merlin Press (1970).
11 *New Left Review,* No. 63.
12 A. Myers, *Solzhenitsyn in Exile,* Pathfinder Press, N.Y. (1974).
13 *Arkhipelag GULag,* YMCA, Paris (1974), Book II, pp. 599–600.
14 *Bodalsya telyonok s dubom, op. cit.,* p. 60.
15 *Ibid.,* p. 117.
16 *Ibid.,* p. 118.
17 *Ibid.,* p. 126.
18 *Ibid.,* p. 402.
19 *Ibid.,* p. 465.
20 *Le Chêne et le Veau,* Seuil, Paris (1975), p. 93.
21 *Bodalsya telyonok s dubom, op. cit.,* p. 134
22 *Ibid.,* p. 159.
23 *Ibid.,* p. 162.
24 *Ibid.,* p. 182.
25 *Ibid.,* p. 193.
26 *Ibid.,* p. 209.
27 *Ibid.,* pp. 239–40.
28 *Ibid.,* p. 241.
29 *Ibid.,* p. 267.
30 *Ibid.,* p. 292.
31 *Ibid.,* p. 295.
32 *Ibid.,* p. 324.
33 *Ibid.,* p. 330.
34 *Ibid.,* pp. 335–6.
35 *Ibid.,* p. 345.
36 *Ibid.,* p. 370.
37 *Ibid.,* p. 375.
38 *Ibid.,* p. 407.
39 *Ibid.,* p. 407.
40 *Ibid.,* p. 423.
41 *Ibid.,* p. 466.

Part One

LITERARY ANALYSIS

2 Soviet society as a prison-house

The *mise-en-scène* of a great deal of Solzhenitsyn's work, such as *The First Circle, One Day in the Life of Ivan Denisovich, The Love-Girl and the Innocent, Gulag Archipelago,* is that of prison. This prison 'atmosphere' has implications which go far beyond the limits of the particular places mentioned. Solzhenitsyn surely intends us to see his works as a depiction of Soviet life as a whole, as, for example, Heinrich Böll has pointed out.[1] The example of Ivan, the glass-blower arrested on a trumped-up charge because his skills are necessary to the 'First Circle' of the Mavrino prison, 'brought it home . . . that as Ivan said, "They can do just what they want."'[2] In a state which can do just as it wants, the whole of the population is effectively enslaved. Moreover, the concept of 'legality' tends to disappear entirely from such a society. Rules, laws and codes can have no independent, predictable status of their own, and there is no rule of law. It is interesting to note that in the Soviet Union since the death of Stalin there has been considerable emphasis on the promotion of 'socialist legality' and the elimination of 'administrative arbitrariness'. The continuing complaints about this may indicate the endemic nature of administrative arbitrariness in the Soviet system; but even if it were to be eliminated entirely, this might not really be a situation which we would recognise as a 'rule of law'. It seems to be a struggle to establish more what the Germans would term a *Rechtstaat* (namely a state in which governmental power is subject to the law), rather than the English ideal of Professor Dicey, who insisted on an even greater measure of individual liberty.

Although this may appear to some people a somewhat abstract discussion of legal theory, to Captain Buinovskü in Denisovich's camp the issue is far from theoretical. Buinovskii at one point challenges the guards, 'You've no right to strip men in the cold. You don't know article 9 of the Criminal Code.' He is soon to be disabused of this notion: 'But they do have the right. They knew the code. You, chum, are the one who doesn't know it.'[3]

In point of fact, the state *is* the law, as Rusanov attempts to explain to his son Yuri in *Cancer Ward*. 'He specially tried to make Yuri understand the organic interrelationship of all levels and all branches of the state's machinery.'⁴

Party control of the courts effectively subjugates the legal order, an important feature of a totalitarian state.⁵ Soviet judicial procedures have a grim element of hypocrisy about them, as is brilliantly portrayed in the mock trial of Prince Igor carried out by the prisoners of Mavrino in *The First Circle*. Particularly ironic is the use of the word 'objectively' to describe the highly subjective and tendentious reasoning, namely that Prince Igor's easy captivity in the hands of the Polovtsians 'objectively . . . was tantamount to accepting a reward . . . for the treacherous surrender of the troops under his command'.⁶ The concept of 'guilt' is similarly debased by the Vyshinskii philosophy of confession. 'The fact that [a prisoner] confessed proves his guilt';⁷ and this is reinforced by the techniques used by the NKVD, MVD, KGB, and so on, to find pretexts for arresting and charging people. These techniques included the unscrupulous utilisation of the point that no-one is totally guiltless in an *absolute* sense. When Rubin protests in *The First Cricle* that to arrest two suspects and then imprison them both, when only one can be charged, is to punish an innocent man, Oskolupov points out, 'Innocent? What d'you mean? . . . Not guilty of anything at all? The security service will sort that one out.'⁸

However, on occasion, this system of fabrication and confessions, extracted from generally innocent people by methods inclusive of torture, breaks down in open court. This happened, for example, in the case of Traicho Kostov,⁹ the Bulgarian 'Titoist', and exposes, if only for a moment, the mendacious nature of the system. Indeed as Solzhenitsyn points out, practically no-one in the prison camps is either guilty of a crime or any sort of threat to society. This is contrary to any theories of reasonably wide currency about the justification of punishment or imprisonment: for example the utilitarian or retributivist arguments for punishment. In fact, in such a situation, one can make no distinction between those in prison and the rest of society. Hence, prison and normal society seem in this sense to have no dividing lines between them, although of course prison life does have some appalling restrictions which are not directly encountered elsewhere.

The sentences themselves are in fact meted out in such a way as to suggest that the crimes themselves are relatively unimportant. For example, a famous engineer, Potapov, who refused to collaborate with the Germans about a dam-building project, got ten years along with those who had in fact collaborated. 'This was Stalin's hallmark, his style – that splendid disregard for differences, that levelling of friends and enemies that make him a unique figure in the whole of human history.'¹⁰ Standard sentences were in fact the norm for anyone charged under the notorious article 58 of the criminal code, which could be used as a pretext for almost anyone (for the text see, for example, *The Great Terror* by R. Conquest, Appendix G). As in *One Day in the Life of Ivan Denisovich*:

> They'd given Kilgas 25 years. Earlier there'd been a spell when people were lucky; everyone to a man got ten years. But from '49 onwards, the standard sentence was 25, irrespective.[11]

This raises the question of the *reasons* for imprisoning people. In one sense, Solzhenitsyn sees the aim as simply a means of imposing arbitrary rule, of crushing and annihilating people who might think of dissension, and terrorising the remainder. *Is* there, then, some general, ideological or even idealistic–Utopian aim to this despotic imposition of power and the crushing of all actual and potential opposition? Solzhenitsyn does not systematically discuss the Marxist vision of communism, but I think that Solzhenitsyn makes one very strong point against the claims that the ultimate ends of the Soviet 'system' were idealistic and humanitarian. The message seems to be that the regime aimed in fact to crush or dehumanise the personality, which explains the implications of the terrible sentence 'in perpetuity'. When Solzhenitsyn asks the caretaker why the ashes of Polonsky had been removed to Riazan ('The ashes of the poet'), 'The warder thought this was a great joke. "Seems he'd done his time – so they let him out." '[12] Prisoners in this society, so it seems near the end of *The First Circle*, can be transported as though they were some kind of carcass, in meat or bread lorries. The sheer numbers of prisoners seem more important than who they might be. When the guards are counting the men in Denisovich's camp, 'No-one dared to make a mistake. If you signed for one head too many, you filled the gap with your own.'[13]

Solzhenitsyn raises the question of how such an appalling tyranny could have arisen. As Shulubin in *Cancer Ward* points out, 'I just can't accept that our whole people suddenly became weak in the head.'[14] He attributes the rise of Stalin's tyranny to the herd instinct, 'the fear of remaining alone, outside the community', which leads on to the 'voluntary acceptance of other people's errors'.[15] However, Lev Leonidovich, the surgeon, attributes complicity in Stalin's crimes to passivity and spinelessness. In defence of a fellow doctor wrongfully accused of negligence, he 'got up and made a speech. . . . How could I have kept silent? If they're putting a noose around your neck, you have to tear it off, there's no point in waiting.'[16] Lev notes with disgust that even in this instance, which occurred after Stalin's death, the chief city surgeon stood up and praised the local party organisation for bringing the trial in public. In some respects this reasoning may indicate a little of Solzhenitsyn's political naïvety. Merle Fainsod has commented that the Soviet system of government does allow for the expression of popular discontent to a limited extent, and he terms the methods of such expression 'lightning rods', conducting popular anger away from society. One example might be the system of complaints.[17] Perhaps in the case of a child's death apparently occurring because of some medical negligence, one can see the local party's motivation for an open trial.

However, Solzhenitsyn's point is that the *reaction* of the party members and the profession is so depressing: this sycophancy is quite useless as a means of preserving one's freedom, since the power of the state effectively resides in the hands of one capricious tyrant, and those who hold any post within the hierarchy owe all their power and freedom of action to his unbridled whim. In one sense, therefore, the prisoner who has lost everything is freer than those, even the highest placed, who have something to lose. As the prisoner Bobynin points out to the powerful Minister Abakumov in *The First Circle*, 'You can tell old you-know-who up there, that you only have power over people so long as you don't take everything away from them.'[18] Certainly, the contrast between Bobynin and the Minister is striking: Abakumov is terrified of Stalin, who could have annihilated him 'at a stroke'. His 'interviews [with Stalin], which lasted about an hour, were a heavy price to pay for all the might and power with which Abakumov was invested. He was only able to enjoy life in between interviews.'[19] Solzhenitsyn compares this with the peace that prisoners enjoy, even when about to be transferred to the Far North: 'They were at peace with themselves. They were as fearless as men are who have lost everything they ever had – a fearlessness hard to attain but enduring once it is reached.'[20]

This fearlessness is hard to attain because, as Solzhenitsyn admits, a prisoner always considers that he has got something more to lose, even when he has been deprived of almost everything. He does not therefore protest adequately until it is too late for the protest to be effective. Nevertheless, the prisoner may still gain advantages which are not possible elsewhere. For example (Solzhenitsyn claims), an awareness of what is depicted as absolutes of good and evil, as experienced by Innokenti Volodin in *The First Circle*. We are told that Innokenti experienced 'bliss' after the ordeal of his surprise arrest and incarceration in the Lubyanka prison, when he realised that he had done the right thing in trying to warn his friend by telephone about the danger of arrest. And 'for Innokenti, good and evil were now absolute and distinct, and visibly separated by the pale grey door in front of him, by those whitewashed walls, by the experience of his first night in prison'.[21] It may be difficult for some to understand Solzhenitsyn's insistence on the absolute and non-relative nature of ethics, and such a view is no doubt attended by much philosophical controversy, little of which is discussed by Solzhenitsyn. However, in the prison context I am reminded of a conversation with a Dutch university teacher, Mrs Catherine Geyl, who told me that during the wartime occupation of Holland it was highly respectable to be in prison, but rather confusing to be 'outside' unless actively engaged in the Resistance.

At the same time, Solzhenitsyn does not overlook the dehumanising aspect of prison, which for example tends to destroy family and married life, because of the system of implicating any relatives of prisoners and discriminating against them in the course of their everyday lives. Hence although many of Solzhenitsyn's characters, such as Alex in *The Candle in the Wind*, can regard the years in prison as 'fruitful',[22] Solzhenitsyn nevertheless deplores the deprivation of these basic rights to people less concerned with the heroic and spiritual experiences of people like Innokenty, or Solzhenitsyn himself. As Fetiukov in Denisovich's camp discovers, although he 'had three children at home, when he was sentenced they'd disclaimed him and his wife had married again. So he got no help from anywhere.'[23] Since few people can stand against the prevailing ethos of society, Solzhenitsyn points out that in the long run, 'these women [wives of prisoners] began really to feel guilty as their husbands did not'.[24] Sometimes this led to a public disavowal of the husband. In a similar context, Kostoglotov in *Cancer Ward* quotes Yesenin's lines, 'The hurricane swept by, few of us survived and many failed to answer friendship's roll call.'

Solzhenitsyn deals with the terrible conflicts involved in marriage to a prisoner, in chapters 36 and 38 of *The First Circle*, and with tremendous pathos he notes the scenes between prisoners and their wives as viewed through the eyes of a warder: 'The regulations did not explicitly forbid the shedding of tears, but, if one went by the spirit of the law, they clearly could not be permitted.'[25]

Solzhenitsyn sees the life of prisoners in *The Love-Girl and the Innocent* as the world of Gulag, 'Campland'. However, he draws parallels between this world and Soviet society as a whole. Two aspects in particular of life in the camps can be seen as comments on Soviet society as a whole: their hierarchies and their economic structure.

In Ivan Denisovich's camp there are all kinds of class distinctions between, for example, the various grades of office workers, such as Der or, lower down, Tsezar, and the labouring 'zeks'. These are artificial classifications, as opposed to the natural differentiation which emerges within Tuirin's team. Solzhenitsyn sees some people as spiritually superior, or at any rate more valuable to society, as compared with others. In another sense, he emphasises the inherent importance of all personalities as individuals. However, his emphasis on the superiority of certain individuals, such as Bobynin in *The First Circle*, verges occasionally upon a kind of Platonism. Why, then, should he object to class differentation in Soviet society? and how is such a view compatible with emphasis on egalitarianism of political rights? In answer to this last question, I believe that Solzhenitsyn would regard the question of political rights as quite distinct from moral, personal or even economic egalitarianism. Secondly, as a true Christian, he would probably not presume to judge a man's worth in the eyes of God. But his complaint about the class differentation in the Soviet system would I think be two-fold. In the first place it is contrary to the declared principles of communism, and in particular to Lenin's 'April Theses'.[26] In the second place the Soviet system, or at least the camp system, tends to so distort the pattern of 'natural' inegalitarianism as to promote into a relatively rigid hierarchy just those who are most worthless, inefficient or corrupt.

For example, the rewards of the system are most unfairly distributed. For the overfulfilment of work norms,

> The camp got thousands of extra roubles ... and so could give higher bonuses to its guard lieutenants, for example to Volkovoi for using his whip. And you? You got an extra two hundred grammes of bread for your supper.[27]

As a contributor to *Grani*, D. Blagov (pseudonym for a close friend of Solzhenitsyn) writes, 'In the camp there is among the "zeks", not to mention the "free" workers, as in some feudal society or the church, a complicated hierarchy of rights and privileges.'[28] To some extent, this picture of prison society has its counterpart elsewhere, for example in the relation of such families as that of Makarygin, the State Prosecutor (*The First Circle*), to the 'common people'. We are told that Clara, the Prosecutor's daughter, lived in evacuation 'out of range of enemy shells and shielded from the horrors of war on the home front'.[29] In the case of the Rusanovs in *Cancer Ward* we encounter people who are careful not to mix too freely with the common people at work, and keen to ensure that their son Yuri does not marry anyone too 'ordinary'. 'They served the People. . . . But as the years went by they found themselves less and less able to tolerate actual human beings. . . .'[30]

The organisation of the camp economy is also complex and inegalitarian. In *One Day in the Life of Ivan Denisovich* there is a long description of how the feeding arrangements are managed by the camp cook who pays off various 'trusties' to do his dirty jobs for him. Some of the officials are largely superfluous, such as the sanitary inspector in the kitchens; but 'that was according to the rules: one man works, one man watches'.[31] As regards the bureaucracy surrounding the performance of work by the prisoners, Shukhov records that 'more depended on the work report than on the work itself'.[32] In short, these had to be falsified to provide the means of subsistence for a work team. Once again there is a parallel with 'life outside', as Matryona records with reference to the local Peat Trust. 'They [kolkhoz women] waste time arguing about the hours they've worked, who's on and who's off.'[33] Such a system produces widespread falsification of returns, for work reports must tally with the record of work completed. Moreover, the low rates of pay and the necessity of bribing various officials in the camps find their counterpart in Matryona's village, for example, where some of the village women have to steal peat to remain warm in the winter. Matryona explains that the Peat Trust 'probably coped with the problem by exaggerating their production figures and then writing off a certain percentage to loss from the effects of rain and crumbling'.[34]

Another parallel between the economic regulation of the camps and that of the country is one mentioned in *The Love-Girl and the Innocent*, where at one point the innovation of installing a bronze foundry is being discussed. This is temporarily rejected by the workers because it will not bring them any more pay, owing to the fact that all payment is made by weight. This method of output and productivity assessment was fairly usual in the planning of the national economy in Stalin's day. When Munitsa, the skilled foundry worker, suggests the construction of a new bronze furnace, his foreman Chegenyov points out,

> Course there won't be any percentage increase. They'll pay for the bronze like they now pay for the cast iron; by weight. An iron girder weighs half a ton, a wheel bush half a kilo. Your furnace'll be the death of us.[35]

Solzhenitsyn has much more to say about such matters as conditions of work in the camps, the use of over-extended work norms which seem designed, at least in part, to crush the human spirit. Even Yakonov, the chief at Mavrino in *The First Circle*, reflects 'The system crushed you, driving you harder and faster all the time, demanding more and more, setting inhuman time limits.'[36] While the total subordination of the trade unions and the imposition of excessive work norms both within and outside the camps during the Stalin era has been convincingly documented in such works as Conquest's *The Great Terror*, and elsewhere, it is less clear that such conditions operate in the same way in the Soviet Union today.

SUMMARY

Solzhenitsyn believes that there has been no 'rule of law' in the Soviet Union, and that the courts are integrated into the state apparatus because the party controls them. He says that few people who were arrested, tried and imprisoned were in fact guilty of an offence. He claims that the standard procedure in courts was to rely on the confessions of the accused, and that these confessions were extracted in many cases by torture. He believes that the system was used by Lenin and Stalin for the purposes of establishing absolute power, and not for any long-term humanitarian aims. He suggests that the Russian and Soviet peoples were themselves to blame for the rise of Soviet power and Stalin; the Russian people were too politically inexperienced, too servile, too ready to compromise in order to preserve their own positions. Solzhenitsyn points out that in such a society no-one is absolutely safe, and there is therefore an element of prison or enslavement about the whole of Soviet society. However, he believes resistance, or a kind of spiritual civil disobedience, is possible, provided the prisoner or the person concerned does not try to preserve power, property or even family ties. He applies the lessons of the camps to Soviet society as a whole, emphasising that their hierarchies and their economic life have much in common with the organisation of Soviet life outside the camps.

NOTES

1   *Merkur*, No. 5 (May 1969), pp. 482–3.
2   *Sob. Soch.*, Vol. 3, p. 341.
3   *Sob. Soch.*, Vol. 1, p. 28.
4   *Sob. Soch.*, Vol. 2, p. 443.
5   L. B. Schapiro, *Totalitarianism*, Macmillan (1972).
6   *Sob. Soch.*, Vol. 4, p. 424.
7   *Ibid.*, p. 512.
8   *Ibid.*, p. 706.
9   *Sob. Soch.*, Vol. 3, p. 20.
10 *Ibid.*, p. 223.
11 *Sob. Soch.*, Vol. 1, p. 51.
12 *Sob. Soch.*, Vol. 5, p. 224.
13 *Sob. Soch.*, Vol. 1, p. 30.
14 *Sob. Soch.*, Vol. 2, p. 481.
15 *Ibid.*, p. 483.
16 *Ibid.*, pp. 406–7.
17 L. B. Schapiro, *The Government and Politics of the Soviet Union*, Hutchinson (1970), pp. 151–2.
18 *Sob. Soch.*, Vol. 3, p. 119.
19 *Ibid.*, p. 142.
20 *Sob. Soch.*, Vol. 4, p. 804.
21 *Ibid.*, p. 746.
22 *Sob. Soch.*, Vol. 5, p. 140.
23 *Sob. Soch.*, Vol. 1, p. 39.
24 *Sob. Soch.*, Vol. 3, p. 214.
25 *Ibid.*, p. 320.
26 Thesis 3 (B) (Lenin's 'April Theses').
27 *Sob. Soch.*, Vol. 1, p. 47.
28 *Sob. Soch.*, Vol. 6, p. 342.
29 *Sob. Soch.*, Vol. 3, p. 329.
30 *Sob. Soch.*, Vol. 2, pp. 220–1.
31 *Sob. Soch.*, Vol. 6, p. 338.
32 *Ibid.*, p. 341.
33 *Sob. Soch.*, Vol. 1, p. 207.

34 *Ibid.*, p. 205.
35 *Sob. Soch.*, Vol. 5, p. 30.
36 *Sob. Soch.*, Vol. 3, p. 169. The Russian drives home the inexorability of this process: 'Vyzhimayushchii bol'she, bystree, eshchyo eshchyo normu sverkh normy, tri normy. . . .'

3 The Gulag Archipelago
(A) Soviet courts and law in theory and practice

The themes explored in the last chapter, including the nature of Soviet law and the depiction of society as various degrees of prison, have been much more fully developed in Solzhenitsyn's *Gulag Archipelago*, which was published in three volumes (seven sections) between December 1973 and March 1976. The first part was published in the most dramatic circumstances: in September 1973, the *Daily Telegraph* reported that

> Alexander Solzhenitsyn claimed yesterday that a woman killed herself after revealing during five days' non-stop interrogation by the KGB, the State Security Police, the existence of a manuscript of a book he had written. The Nobel Prize-winning author named the woman as Yelizaveta Voronyanskaya, and said that her interrogation was carried out in Leningrad. 'When she returned home she hanged herself,' he said, but gave no further details. . . . Entitled *Arkhipelag GULag* it is about Stalinist labour camps.[1]

Only one aspect of this report is incorrect. The work is about Soviet camps, mainly during 1918–56, but it includes some information about Brezhnev's rule as well, thus covering the period from Lenin to the sixties. Solzhenitsyn thus indicts not only the Stalinist era but effectively the whole post-revolutionary era. On occasions he has apparently believed that the appearance of his work will shake the Soviet state to its foundations: 'In this seizure [of the manuscript] I saw the hand of God, and realised the time had come. As Macbeth was told: Birnam Wood will walk.'[2] Solzhenitsyn had taken the precaution of smuggling a microfilm copy of his work abroad, and he compared its publication to the famous scene near the end of *Macbeth* when the downfall of the illegal regime is signalled by the approach of Macduff's camouflaged army.

Solzhenitsyn has described his publication as 'an attempted artistic evaluation' of the period 1918–56. It is based on the testimony of 227 witnesses as well as Solzhenitsyn's own experiences. Many people have agreed about its overall accuracy and truth, including R. Medvedev[3] and A. Sakharov.[4] The reaction of the Soviet authorities seems to suggest that this is so, whereas those who deny its objectivity, such as Solzhenitsyn's former wife Reshetovskaya, seem implausible.[5] Reshetovskaya has written that Solzhenitsyn was selective in his use of evidence, and that the evidence was based on hearsay. However, Reshetovskaya does not apparently feel confident enough to state that the 'hearsay' was untrue. She does not attempt to rebut the charges against the regime which Solzhenitsyn's massive evidence, even if it is selective evidence, clearly establishes.

In one sense Solzhenitsyn has not been selective enough, and his work is as vast and incoherent as the shocking events he describes. Yet he has written a work of scholarship which is at the same time a triumph of the human spirit over suffering and death. Let those who deny its accuracy or its conclusions come forward with convincing proof: so far none has appeared.

Solzhenitsyn compared the whole concentration camp system controlled by the MVD's (Ministry of Internal Affairs) Main Camp Administration (Gulag) to a country 'with the torn geography of an archipelago but with the cohesive psychology of a continent – the almost invisible and almost intangible country which the prison people settled'.[6] However, Solzhenitsyn does also stress most emphatically that the Gulag Archipelago has had a profound effect on the whole of Soviet society. It is almost impossible for the Western mind to grasp the scope and extent of the Gulag Archipelago. In 1929–30, we are told that 15 million peasants ('kulaks') were deported in the collectivisation campaign and forced to work in camps in the tundra and taiga of Siberia. Solzhenitsyn also describes the wave of arrests in 1937–8 as a 'Volga' of national grief. And afterwards,

> came the stream of 1945–6, as big as the good Yenisei: whole nations were forced through the sewage pipes, along with million upon million of others who . . . had been in prison, had been deported to Germany and then returned.[7]

Solzhenitsyn refers here to the deportation of such nations as the Crimean Tartars and the Volga Germans, and to the Soviet troops imprisoned in Germany, all of whom were suspected by Stalin of collaboration with the Nazis. Quite explicitly, Solzhenitsyn traces the origins of these camps back to the first concentration camp on the Solovetskii Islands, and to practises originating in the Civil War period and before under Lenin and Dzerzhinskii. The basic illegality, terror and hostility to democracy started with Lenin: it was Lenin, after all, who urged first 'the purging of all harmful insects from the Russian soil' ('harmful insects' included 'every worker who shirked his job').[8] It was Lenin who wrote in a letter to Kurskii, People's Commissar of Justice, in May 1922,

'It is also necessary to extend the practice of execution by shooting . . .';[9] and it was Lenin, as early as August 1918, before the attempt on his life by Fanny Kaplan, who wrote to Yevgenia Bosh, 'Lock up all the doubtful ones [!] in a concentration camp [kontslager]'.[10] Solzhenitsyn points out that it was therefore Lenin who was first in the twentieth century to advocate such measures against citizens of his own country.

In this book it will be necessary to analyse Lenin's legacy beginning in 1917. However, it will also be necessary to limit the discussion to certain themes, for it is quite impossible to do justice to this mighty work in the space available.* The themes I have chosen, and which seem to me to be most important, are as follows:

(A) Soviet courts and law in theory and practice
(B) Soviet penology in theory and practice
(C) Soviet camps and their effect on Soviet society.

In the first years of the revolution, there were three kinds of courts: the People's Courts, the Circuit Courts and the Revolutionary Tribunals (Revtribs). The People's Courts had limited powers, but their maximum sentences were raised to ten years (minimum: six months) in 1922. Their decision could be raised by government intervention. The other courts could impose any sentences up to and including the death penalty, with only a brief let-up (Circuit Courts in 1920, Revtribs in 1921). From very early in the post-revolutionary period, however, these courts had limited autonomy. According to People's Prosecutor N. V. Krylenko, the Government (VTsIK) 'pardons and punishes, at its own discretion, without any limitation whatever'.[11] This, said Krylenko, showed the superiority of the revolutionary judicial system over the false theory of the separation of powers. Krylenko went on to say that the court is 'at one and the same time both the creator of law and a political weapon'.[12] In 1938, the 'political weapon' of the court was to be used against Krylenko himself, and Solzhenitsyn makes the point that those who defend illegality, even if their reasoning is based on impeccable Marxist principles, cannot expect legal treatment themselves. Krylenko, indeed, piled the lethal concepts one upon another: 'A tribunal is an organ of the class struggle of the workers directed against their enemies.'[13] 'Class expediency', it seemed, was the vital factor, not guilt. The concept of guilt was an old bourgeois concept (said Krylenko) which had now been uprooted.[14] He went on to say,

And it must also be borne in mind that it was not what he had done that constituted the defendant's burden, but what he might do if he

---

* I feel confident that the *Gulag Archipelago* will become the subject of a vast literature as well as being influential in determining some of the future long-term developments in the Soviet polity.

were not shot now. We protect ourselves not only against the past, but also against the future.[15]

Solzhenitsyn's point is that neither Krylenko nor any jurist who upholds these principles can protect himself in the future, for if courts have such powers, literally no-one is safe.

Solzhenitsyn takes us through many of the famous trials of the 1920s and 1930s in order to show how features of Soviet practice developed under the influence of both Marxist legal theory and Krylenko's formulations. He points out that in a court or tribunal where neither the letter of the law nor the supposed offence of the accused is under discussion but rather his class origins, his attitude to the revolution and his 'expediency' or 'inexpediency' to the state, the role of the defence becomes minimal, while the scope of the state's powers become maximal.

At the trial of the Orthodox Church leaders in March 1922 (Tikhon) and June–July 1922 (Veniamin and others), threats were made by the court to arrest the principal defence lawyer (Bobrishchev-Pushkin), while one defence witness (Professor Yegorov) was actually arrested 'because of his testimony on behalf of the Metropolitan'.[16] Other features of the trial are noteworthy: the supposedly public courtroom was 'packed' with a selected audience, and Solzhenitsyn pointed out that this happened not only at the famous trials of 1937 but also at trials in 1968 (Ginsberg and Galanskov?). Moreover, the phrase 'enemy of the people' was used, and libellous innuendo was stirred up in the press to the effect that not only had the churchmen failed to relieve famine in the Volga region (by sale of church treasures) but also the church was therefore to some extent responsible. Solzhenitsyn makes the point that the laws of the state must have some limits, and that the church should have been allowed to donate voluntarily rather than being compelled. Ten churchmen were condemned to death, and four were shot in August 1922.

Lenin apparently intervened in a number of trials. He amended the Criminal Code of 1922 to raise the number of capital crimes from six to twelve, and he advocated terror 'as a method of persuasion'.[17] An important part of Lenin's proposed amendments to the Criminal Code was the section which later became part of article 58: 'propaganda or agitation, or participation in an organisation, or assistance [objectively assisting or being capable of assisting] . . . organisations or persons whose activity has the character . . . [of being anti-Soviet].'[18] Solzhenitsyn points out that under such a formulation it would be possible to find literally anyone guilty, and that the law was specifically used for this purpose.

The trial of the Socialist Revolutionary Party leaders, held later in 1922, also revealed certain characteristics of the Soviet regime. The court equated the *de facto* seizure of power by the Bolsheviks with a legal accession to power. Hence the actions of the SRs in opposing this were *illegal*, as was their subsequent opposition to the dispersal of the Constituent Assembly ('elected by free, equal, secret, and direct voting'[19]) in January 1918. Similarly the demand of the SRs for new election to the Soviets, with freedom for all parties to engage in electoral campaigning, was depicted as an irresponsible suggestion, perhaps even treacherous, because the new regime was still encircled by enemies. This was to become a perennial argument for internal suppression.

The Central Committee of the SR Party had apparently failed to denounce their supporters who were planning to organise political activity against the Bolsheviks. Krylenko held that the fact that these intentions had not been carried out was of 'no essential significance'[20] and that the failure to denounce was itself a crime.[21] One of the defendants in the case, Gendelman-Grabovskii, had the temerity to suggest that the witnesses had been tampered with by the GPU (secret police, successors to the Cheka). Krylenko said at this stage that the court's investigation was much more important than the preliminary enquiry, but later the confession of defendants at the preliminary 'enquiry' became the *only* source of evidence before Soviet courts.* Finally, in this case, while fourteen defendants were shot, the sentences of the remainder were not implemented, being dependant on the actions of Socialist Revolutionaries in general. Thus the survivors were held by the regime as hostages.

Solzhenitsyn quotes cases in which certain other notable features of Soviet legal practice arose. In the case of B. V. Savinkov (1924), some totally absurd charges were pinned on the accused, who had voluntarily returned to Russia from a period abroad. These were 'assisting the Russian bourgeoisie in carrying out its imperialist ambitions'. The sentence was made to seem lenient for reasons of diplomacy, and finally the prisoner was killed in the Lubyanka and a faked suicide note was left.[22] Here Solzhenitsyn highlights the covert illegality of the authorities, if considered necessary to achieve their real aims.

After 1926, those who were 'inexpedient' to the regime could be charged under article 58 (mentioned above) of the revised Criminal Code, while yet another category of crime began to appear. This was the implausible crime of 'wrecking'. For example, the Chief Engineer of Moscow's water supply, V. V. Oldenberger, was supposed to have sabotaged his own system, making use of 'centres' for this purpose. The regime thus began to find scapegoats for economic failures in extraordinary numbers, including engineers in the Shakhty case (May–July 1928) and the Industrial Party trial ('Prompartiya', whose trial occurred

---

* Krylenko's directives became binding on the whole judicial system.

in November–December 1930). The report of this trial can be read to this day,[23] and contained a deliberately confusing mass of detail, designed to substantiate some absurd charges, namely that the 'Prom-party' prepared the way for the intervention of foreign powers in the Civil War, took money from the imperialists, conducted espionage and assigned posts in a future government. Surely no-one today need discuss the plausibility of these charges, but Solzhenitsyn does agree that there was a community of interest between the engineers at the time. This community of interest, as interpreted by Solzhenitsyn, says something about his view of political parties. He suggests that the engineers were faced with damaging government policies during War Communism, the NEP and the first five-year plan. So they tended to work together.

> But they didn't need any kind of conference, any membership cards, to achieve such unity. Like every kind of mutual understanding between intelligent and clear-thinking people, it was attained by a few quiet, even accidental words; no voting was called for. Only narrow minds need resolutions and the Party stick.[24]

The government, needing a scapegoat for the failures induced by its crazy tempo of economic development, turned on the engineers.

During this trial, once again some essential characteristics of Soviet legal practice began to appear. In answer to suggestions that the witnesses and the defendants had been tampered with before the trial, Krylenko countered: 'why were they arrested and why did they all at once start babbling their heads off?' He went on to say, 'Why did they confess? And I ask you, what else could they have done?'[25] The answers must be: arrest should not presuppose guilt, and babblings and confessions can be extracted by torture. The defendants hoped that by cooperating they would receive mercy, and this helped to sustain defendants in subsequent trials and to guarantee the success of these trials, at least up to the treacherous murder of Zinoviev and Kamenev.[26]

The trials of the 1930s therefore became forms of carefully scripted plays, 'according to the wishes of the Chief Producer' – i.e. Stalin.[27] It seems from the evidence that one of the gravest weaknesses of those defendants who agreed to confess, and to those witnesses who testified according to the 'prepared script', was that they were *trying to cooperate*. It is essential, says Solzhenitsyn, to realise that no cooperation or compromise is possible. He cites the case of N. I. Bukharin, who in his last letter 'to the Future Central Committee' begged to be restored to the party and said that he fully approved of everything that had happened up to and including 1937. 'And that is how he himself certified that he too deserved to plunge into those waves.'[28] He says that the only firm stand which those who were tried in 1922, 1924, in the 1930s and in the post-war period was: 'No, we are not Russians with you! No, we are not Communists with you!'[29]

Some people proved firm in the face of this judicial persecution. Solzhenitsyn cites the case of communists Smirnov, Univer, Saburov and Vlasov in the remote town of Kady near Ivanovo in the late thirties. They were supposed to have been responsible for failures in bread distribution, but Vlasov in particular conducted himself in such a way that the public at his trial opposed the death sentence, and he had to be taken to Ivanovo to await his execution. After waiting in the most lugubrious circumstances for his sentence over a period of 41 days, Vlasov's sentence was commuted to twenty years in corrective labour camps. His final comment was

> It is strange. I was condemned for lack of faith in the victory of socialism in our country. But can Kalinin* himself believe in it if he thinks that camps will still be needed in our country twenty years from now?[30]

Camps were still needed after thirty years.

In discussing the judicial practice of the Soviet Union as it evolved in the pre-war period, it is necessary not to overlook the *extra*-judicial practices of the secret police. The Cheka ('The Extraordinary Committee for the struggle against counter-revolution and sabotage') was set up by Lenin and Bonch-Bruevich in December 1917. It was the forerunner of all subsequent organs of extrajudicial repression in the Soviet Union, namely the GPU, the OGPU, the NKVD, the MVD and the KGB of today. According to Solzhenitsyn, the Cheka was 'the only punitive organ in human history to concentrate in its own hands the functions of detections, arrest, investigation, prosecution, trial, and implementation of sentence.'[31] In Lenin's 'Regulations for Revolutionary Tribunals'[32] we find that the Cheka was empowered to execute prisoners for belonging to the 'exploiting class' or merely to 'deter the enemies of the revolution'. Such class enemies could be located and shot at 'the behest of [the Chekist's] revolutionary conscience'. Solzhenitsyn uses two major sources, Latsis and Gernet,[33] to show that in the eighteen months after the revolution, the Cheka shot on average three times as many people per month as had been executed at the height of Tsarist repression under Prime Minister Stolypin in 1906–7, a period of six months. As a result of these extraordinary powers, people often agreed to become informers to avoid punishment. Moreover, the Cheka had powers to instigate terror 'to deter the enemies of the revolution'. They were also directed to instigate 'popular wrath' against the accused in certain important trials'.[34] Solzhenitsyn says that

---

* At that time Kalinin was President of the USSR.

By the time of the [Industrial Party] trial of November to December 1930, this meant general meetings, demonstrations (involving even school children), the heavy tread of millions and the roar outside the courthouse windows: 'Death! Death! Death!'[35]

A most important point is made here by Solzhenitsyn. At the time, these executions received the unanimous approval of the army commanders, the party leaders and the famous revolutionaries, who 'welcomed the mob's roar, never suspecting that . . . their names would soon figure in that same roar'.[36] Solzhenitsyn is saying in effect that justice and legality are indivisible: those who participate in or approve of injustice have no claims on justice themselves. Moreover in one sense they are themselves guilty of the offences against the innocent. But Solzhenitsyn does not simply condemn in a negative way those who approved, those who failed to speak out, or even those who perpetrated injustice. He asks instead that they now acknowledge their guilt, for this is the only way to build a more just, more legal society in the future.

Judicial persecution and extra-judicial repression did not alter *fundamentally* in the post-war period and the fifties and sixties. The post-war influx into the 'Gulag Archipelago' was perhaps the most chaotic and arbitrary of all. In Part V of the *Gulag Archipelago* Solzhenitsyn points out that a new category of crime sprang up, that of (technical) treason. This crime was supposedly committed by whole national groups, such as the Volga Germans and the Crimean Tartars, and all Russians imprisoned by Germany, since Stalin was suspicious of them all. In 1945–6 a whole new 'continent' sprang up in the Gulag Archipelago.[37] Solzhenitsyn records that the volume of prisoners was so great that sometimes the files pertaining to prisoners got mixed up, so that people served sentences for each other's equally imaginary crimes.[38] He mentions that in most of the camps, kangaroo courts were in operation, in which prisoners meted out sentences to informers, often in the form of murder. He remarks bitterly that these kangaroo courts made fewer mistakes than the state 'troikas', tribunals, military collegia and OSOs (Special Courts) which operated at this time.[39]

Solzhenitsyn states with certainty that Soviet law has fallen into disrepute among ordinary people,[40] and that silence and lack of information and discussion about the Gulag Archipelago are dangerous. He says that the reforms and liberalisation which occurred under Khrushchev, such as the rehabilitations of 1956 and the changes in the Criminal Code of 1958, were only partial. Changes of terminology, for example calling political prisoners 'criminals',[41] do not alter the basic injustice. He points out that Soviet law today is anomalous in that it favours perjurers (in the state interest) and can prosecute people via retroactive legislation. Yet in selected cases (Criminal Code of 1961, reducing maximum sentence to fifteen years) this rule did not apply, for example to those serving 25-year sentences. Most important of all, however, is the fact that the whole edifice of law, courts and trials is really a façade. The real decisions are taken in party circles, and courts and prosecutors are merely the obedient servants. Solzhenitsyn concludes, 'A powerful State towers over its second half century, embraced by hoops of steel. The hoops are there indeed but *not* the law.'[42]

Solzhenitsyn thus points out that there is no guarantee that judicial murder and terror, as well as illegal secret police action, will not again become possible in the USSR. And people should not be duped by the fact that the Gulag Archipelago today contains not millions, as under Stalin, but only tens of thousands. Above all it is necessary to change public opinion in the USSR, which contrary to Western illusions no longer supports Soviet law. Solzhenitsyn says that this can only come about by radical changes, and he considers them necessary because he believes that a state without the support of public opinion must fall, just as the Tsarist system had 'sickened from within' well before the defeat of Kolchak or even the February revolution of 1917.[43]

SUMMARY

This chapter deals with the development of Soviet judicial and legal practice, and of extra-judicial repression, under the influence of Marxist theory, Lenin and Krylenko. It shows that these influences continue in principle to this day. From the beginning, the conduct of trials has always been subject to intervention by party and government, thus eliminating the separation of powers. Public opinion acquiesced at an early stage in these practices, and the public was manipulated by the authorities to give some kind of legitimacy to draconian sentences. Hence the public itself and all those who approved, in effect *themselves* laid the basis for their own enslavement. The case of N. I. Bukharin, whose last writings approved of all that had been taking place up to 1937, is an example of this point.

Solzhenitsyn shows how the concept of the 'guilt' of the accused was abandoned as a bourgeois concept, but was replaced by a much more lethal idea, namely that of the *potential* danger or 'inexpediency' of the accused to the state. In a court which is used as a political weapon, the role of the defence becomes minimal and the rights of the defence witnesses tenuous. Moreover a state which uses courts in this way tends also to equate legality with the strength required to obtain political power and to maintain it.

Solzhenitsyn points out that the practice of 'working over' the defendants and witnesses before a major trial began early in the 1920s, as did the practice of regarding confessions by the accused as the best form of evidence. He shows that courts were used as a means of conducting diplomacy and sometimes holding hostages. Absurd charges such as 'wrecking' were pinned on the apparently guilty accused as a means of diverting attention from government failures and providing scapegoats. This practice also created an atmosphere of mutual suspicion and mistrust, in which the discovery of subversive groups such as the 'Industrial Party' became plausible. Solzhenitsyn shows that such groups did not exist in the normal sense of a political party, or else that they were totally fictitious; a fact of which prosecutor, judges and interrogators were usually well aware. This reduced Soviet trials to some kind of carefully scripted play acting. In case some of the accused 'actors' might prove reluctant to play their parts, they were often tortured in order to break their wills and capacity for independent thought. Solzhenitsyn agrees that it is very difficult, but suggests that it is not impossible, to resist such treatment. However, any attempts to negotiate or compromise with the authorities proved to be a recipe for failure.

Solzhenitsyn also draws attention to the fact that the extra-judicial powers of the Cheka were in operation from at least 1918, and that they included the death penalty which was used much more readily than at the height of Tsarist repression. Lenin's influence on the extension of the death penalty, the use of terror and the shaping of the Criminal Code are also recorded.

Judicial and extra-judicial repressions have continued throughout the post-war period, although today the Gulag Archipelago is much smaller than it was under Stalin. Solzhenitsyn believes that the supposed liberalisation under Khrushchev did not alter the fundamental characteristic of the system, and that there is no guarantee that the repressions have ceased for ever. He draws attention to the fact of selective retroactive legislation, the use of manipulated witnesses, the continuing use of illegal KGB methods, and the fact that party control reduces the judicial edifice to a sham in which public opinion no longer has confidence.

NOTES
1 *Daily Telegraph* (7 September 1973).
2 *The Times* (21 January 1974).
3 R. Medvedev, in L. Labedz (ed.), *Solzhenitsyn – a Documentary Record*, Pelican (1974), pp. 372–3.
4 A. Sakharov, in *ibid.*, p. 364.
5 N. Reshetovskaya, in *The Last Circle*, Novosti, Moscow (1974), p. 135.
6 I. Szenfeld, *Radio Liberty Research Bulletin* (15 March 1974), p. 7.
7 *Ibid.*, p. 10.
8 *Ibid.*, p. 11.
9 *Ibid.*

10   *Arkhipelag GULag*, Parts III–IV, YMCA, Paris (1974), p. 17.
11   N. V. Krylenko, *Za Pyat Let.* (1918–22), p. 13.
12   *Ibid.*, p. 3.
13   *Ibid.*, p. 73.
14   *Ibid.*, p. 318.
15   *Ibid.*, p. 82.
16   *Gulag Archipelago*, Parts I–II, Fontana (1974), p. 354.
17   Lenin, *Sobranie Sochinenii*, Vol. 39, pp. 404–5.
18   *Gulag Archipelago*, Parts I–II, *op. cit.*, p. 354.
19   *Ibid.*, p. 356.
20   *Ibid.*, p. 364.
21   *Ibid.*, p. 363.
22   *Ibid.*, p. 368.
23   *Protsess Prompartii*, Sovetskoe Zakonodatelstvo, Moscow (1931).
24   *Gulag Archipelago*, Parts I–II, *op. cit.*, p. 392.
25   *Ibid.*, p. 394.
26   *Ibid.*, p. 397.
27   *Ibid.*, p. 391.
28   *Ibid.*, p. 417.
29   *Ibid.*, p. 419.
30   *Ibid.*, p. 455.
31   *Radio Liberty Research Bulletin*, *op. cit.*, p. 11.
32   *Sobranie Uzakonenii*, 13 (1919), chapter VII, para. 22.
33   M. Latsis, *Dva Goda Borby na Vnutrennom Fronte*, Moscow (1920); M. N. Gernet (ed.), *Protiv Smertnoi Kazni*, Moscow (1907), pp. 385–423.
34   *Radio Liberty Research Bulletin*, *op. cit.*, p. 13.
35   *Ibid.*
36   *Ibid.*, p. 14.
37   *Arkhipelag GULag*, Parts V–VII, YMCA, Paris (1976), p. 39.
38   *Gulag Archipelago*, Parts I–II, *op. cit.*, p. 559.
39   *Arkhipelag GULag*, Parts V–VII, *op. cit.*, p. 248.
40   *Ibid.*, pp. 528–9.
41   *Ibid.*, p. 556.
42   *Ibid.*, pp. 576–8.
43   *Ibid.*, p. 99.

4 *The Gulag Archipelago* (B) Soviet penology in theory and practice

Solzhenitsyn suggests that the Gulag Archipelago originated in the 'Temporary instruction on the deprivation of freedom', issued after the 'July coup' on 23 July 1918. It read, 'Those deprived of freedom who are capable of labour must be recruited for work on a compulsory basis.' However, although the practice of forced labour camps was founded in the civil war, it was not until 1921 that the Northern Special Purpose Camps (SLON) were founded. The Solovetskii Islands in the White Sea are singled out by Solzhenitsyn for special attention.

The Solovetskii Islands (Solovki) were largely monastic lands, and the Soviet authorities set up a prison based on the monastery buildings. Here, former White Guards and members of the aristocracy were imprisoned, as well as criminals. Solzhenitsyn describes how prisoners were shot here as early as the first years of the 1920s. It is true that many were officers of the White Armies, but this practice was soon extended to others. The use of forced labour to crush prisoners also began here, especially the use of logging parties in the more remote parts of Solovki. Solzhenitsyn comments, 'At that time too they "discovered" the device of new work parties which consisted of sending several hundred people to totally unprepared uninhabitable places.'[1] Solzhenitsyn describes the collaboration of the first camp guards, themselves White Guards, with the Chekists. But this should not be all that surprising, he says, except to

> someone used to social analysis on a class basis and unable to see differently. But to such an analyst everything in the whole world is bound to be astonishing, because the whole world and human beings never fit into his previously set little grooves.[2]

Although Solzhenitsyn goes as far as to describe Solovki as 'an Arctic Auschwitz',[3] it seems that it was only a beginning of a whole series of 'metastases' which spread out many ways throughout the USSR. Solzhenitsyn dwells at considerable length on the construction of the 'Belomor' (White–Baltic Sea) Canal. He suggests that this canal, which was built by armies of prisoners without adequate technology, was far too shallow to take submarines and therefore could not be very useful militarily. (It is only about 16 feet deep in many places.) He compares its construction by 'shock workers' to the Great Leap Forward in China (1958), and seems to be saying that such forced tempos of development are characteristic of communist regimes in general: moreover he is saying that the motive for such constructions is political or penal rather than economic or military. The descriptions of work conditions on the Belomor canal are hair-raising, particularly the use of differential rations as a means of extracting high work norms and dividing the prisoners against each other. This was apparently the invention of a man who rose high in Stalin's camp system, N. Frenkel; and it was used extensively throughout the Gulag Archipelago. Many 'elesi'* and 'zeks'† actually perished in the harsh conditions, and their bones can sometimes be found to this day, says Solzhenitsyn, embedded in the concrete of the canal. The camps were used, it seems, as a means of suppressing their inmates rather than as an efficient means of production. This fact shows up Soviet penology as exceptionally (if characteristically) hypocritical.

In this context, Solzhenitsyn quotes in particular from two works: one by A. Y. Vyshinskii,[4] and one by his pupil I. L. Averbakh.[5] Their theory goes back both to Marx's *Critique of the Gotha Programme*, which advocated the use of productive labour for criminals, and to the 8th Party Congress, which resolved to 'replace the system of punishments with a system of education'.[6] Vyshinskii and Averbakh develop these ideas to insist on *compulsory* education of the prisoner through productive labour in the collective (team work is vital) which is described as a 'driving belt' from the administration to the masses. Averbakh claims that the collective is an example of the spontaneous initiative of the prisoners involved, and that the work performed by such people in such a team is a means towards heightening their moral dignity. Averbakh goes on to make the 'progressive'-sounding claim that such people cannot be subject to moral repression, which is typical of bourgeois prisons. (He does however add the proviso that 'whoever does not work does not eat'.) Productivity was therefore aided by 'socialist competition and the shock-worker movement', stimulated by 'the entire system of rewards'. Fantastic claims were made for the productivity and fervour of those involved in the construction of the canal: for example, of work brigades who voluntarily went to work two hours before time, staying behind to work at the end of the workday; or of 'Stakhanovite' workers who suddenly 'decided' to overfulfil their production norms by a factor of five.[7] These claims were received with enthusiasm, not only by a

* A term used before 1934 (people 'deprived of freedom').
† A term used after 1934 (people 'imprisoned').

sizeable team of Soviet writers, including M. Gorkii and A. Tolstoi, who visited (carefully selected) parts of the canal in the 1930s, but also by leftist opinion in the West.

What Vyshinskii and Averbakh were saying amounted to the following: capitalist countries had been in the habit of punishing people who, because of unfortunate social and economic circumstances, had committed 'crimes' for which they were made to feel guilty and deprived both of freedom and of useful occupation. The new socialist order denied the concept of 'guilt'. It was much too progressive to punish. It insisted on productive activity for prisoners. It replaced wicked bourgeois coercion with compulsory education (or 'reforging') through productive labour in the collective brigade, which both provided a driving belt between the administration and the masses and represented a spontaneous initiative on their part for psychological enrichment and the heightening of human dignity, replacing the system of bourgeois coercion with socialist competition and shock-work, which is stimulated both by material incentives and by popular fervour.

Solzhenitsyn shows what all this really meant in practice: Compulsory imprisonment of all those of whom the state disapproved and their suppression by crippling norms in a group which deprived them of all privacy and crushed work out of them, representing the end of all personal initiative, psychological development and human dignity, [in most cases] replacing the system of bourgeois punishment for crime with inhuman work loads, stimulated by the threat of starvation and forced participation in mass meetings. This, surely, is a prime example of Solzhenitsyn's point that Soviet Marxism is dangerous because its enslaving implications are so well disguised. He bemoans the fact that it is not only the West which seems unwilling to learn from this terrible experience: in Russia, too, 'no-one in our country ever remembers anything, for memory is the Russian's weak spot, especially memory of the bad'.[8] And the Belomor Canal was by no means the worst experience in this respect: Solzhenitsyn shows how camp conditions became even worse at the beginning of the second five-year plan, and worse again in 1938–9, when the numbers in Soviet prisons and camps became so great that orders came to decrease the number of prisoners, often by shooting as in the 'Garanin' and 'Kashketin' executions at Kolyma and Vorkuta.[9] In one way, conditions grew even worse during the war, not only in a material sense, but also because 'the war even did away with the protest inside the soul'.[10]

One remaining problem for Soviet penology is surely the point that if one does away with the concept of 'guilt' of a prisoner, then how can one 'correct' him or her, and what is imprisonment for anyway? Solzhenitsyn quotes P. Stuchka on this last point.[11] Punishment, it seems, is merely a 'measure of social defence'. Vyshinskii regards criminal elements as a legacy of the old society (which was still thought blame-worthy right up to 1952). So he regarded as necessary the use of correc-tive labour camps in order to 'localise and render harmless the criminal elements of the old society'. He talks about the dialectical principle of 'suppression plus re-education' of 'anyone who can be re-educated' (those who could not be re-educated were presumably to be destroyed).[12] Solzhenitsyn points out that these tracts of penology were not published in great numbers: they were simply meant for Soviet diplomats, inter-national congresses and the progressive West, which was almost univer-sally taken in by it all – for example, Supreme Court Judge Leibowitz of New York State.[13] Solzhenitsyn expostulates:

> And oh, you well-fed, devil-may-care, near-sighted irresponsible foreigners with your notebooks and your ball-point pens – beginning with those correspondents who back in Kem asked the zeks questions in the presence of the camp chiefs – how much you have harmed us in your vain passion to shine with understanding in areas where you did not grasp a lousy thing![14]

One area of illusion which seems to persist in the West is that while conditions in the Soviet Union were bad for many years, they were a definite improvement on the Tsarist period. Solzhenitsyn attempts to dispel that illusion. Under the *Normative Statutes* for Tsarist prisons (1869), the working day for prisoners involved in hard labour was laid down as seven hours for logging work and for all kinds of winter work, whereas the maximum for the summer was twelve-and-a-half hours. Moreover these norms were discretionary, since special allowance could be made for the strength of the worker and the degree to which he was accustomed to manual labour. But in the Gulag Archipelago, for example at Karlag in the far North, the summer norms were thirteen to sixteen hours a day, and no allowances were made for individuals.[15] A. Chekhov's report on conditions in the Sakhalin prisons at the end of the nineteenth century showed that prisoners working on roads and in mines during the months of most work re-ceived each day fifty-six ounces of bread, fourteen ounces of meat, and eight and three-quarter ounces of cereal. On the Gulag Archipelago, *shock-worker rations* were twenty-four-and-a-half ounces of inferior bread. Solzhenitsyn goes on to say: 'And the conscientious Chekhov investi-gated whether these norms were really enough! . . . if he had looked into the bowl of a Soviet slogger he would have given up the ghost.'[16]

Moreover, prisoners did not of course receive pay, or much attention to their special abilities. Once again, Solzhenitsyn counterposes Marxist theory with one aspect of Soviet reality: Marx had lashed out at capitalist society for demeaning the professions by its emphasis on the 'naked cash nexus'. 'The bourgeoisie has stripped of its halo every occupation hitherto honoured and looked up to with reverent awe. It has converted the physician, the lawyer, the priest, the poet, the man of science, into its paid wage labourers.'[17] Solzhenitsyn responds:

> Well at least they were paid! And at least they were left to work in their own field on professional specialisation! And what if they had been sent out on *general work*? To logging? And unpaid! And unfed! . . . [Maybe physicians were an exception.] But as for lawyers, priests, poets, and men of science . . . they were only fit to rot doing general work.[18]

Solzhenitsyn goes on to draw convincing parallels between the fate of pre-Emancipation serfs in Russia and Soviet prisoners. Apart from the fact that serfs were in bondage from birth, all the differences between Soviet zeks and serfs were to the discredit of the Gulag Archipelago.[19]

Persecution of prisoners did not, however, cease even after the termination of their sentence. The regulations seemed to discriminate against ex-prisoners, who according to Soviet penal theory had just been 'reforged'. In the post-war period especially, the habit was established of sending ex-prisoners into exile, where they were treated as second-class citizens. No rights to paid vacations or rest days were granted, and the only employment which they could get, often on a state farm or a kolkhoz, was comparable with camp conditions. Exiles felt that they had been 'tainted' by their time in the camps, and that they had been labelled as an enemy for the rest of their lives.[20] This label also affected their personal relations, for since they could get no work without a registration card, and had no bread ration card, they were often avoided by their friends and relatives.[21] The warning given to one prisoner on release, 'Don't imagine you're a free citizen',[22] was not given without reason. Even when an ex-prisoner or an exile was formally rehabilitated, the feeling persisted that this indicated not so much lack of guilt as that the crime had not been a serious one.[23] Those who married ex-prisoners were effectively discriminated against.[24] For all these reasons the natural reaction of the ex-prisoner was to try to forget that his imprisonment ever happened. Solzhenitsyn insists however that it is wrong (and impossible) to forget, since only a careful analysis of the gross injustice of the Soviet penal system which allowed this to happen will enable the country to heal its wounds.[25]

Solzhenitsyn noted the coincidence that he completed the last part of the *Gulag Archipelago* in February 1967, 50 years after the revolution which created the camps, and 100 years after the discovery of barbed wire.[26]

SUMMARY

Solzhenitsyn argues that Soviet penology and penal institutions are based on Marxist ideas of putting prisoners to productive labour, and that these were developed by Vyshinskii and Averbakh. The practical side of labour camps and concentration camps may be seen as originating in the Solovetskii Islands in the White Sea, spreading out from there to many parts of the Soviet Union by the 1930s and 40s. Solzhenitsyn reports the use of differential rations as a means of extracting high work norms, together with extensive collective pressure and mutual informing by prisoners. Crazy work tempos and Stakhanovite efforts in order to achieve results of doubtful economic and strategic value are recorded, together with corrective labour in harsh conditions which often resulted in death. All this was glossed over not only by 'progressive'-sounding justifications which satisfied world opinion in the thirties, but also by deliberate concealment of evidence (a policy continued to this day, as shown by the attempts of the Soviet authorities to stifle publication of the *Gulag Archipelago*).

Solzhenitsyn destroys any lingering belief that conditions in Soviet jails and camps were better than in Tsarist times, and he argues forcefully that the latter were more lenient, taking account of individual abilities and the personalities of prisoners. He claims that conditions for the pre-Emancipation Russian serfs were, in almost every respect, better than those of Soviet prisoners 100 years later. He claims further that 'reforged' ex-prisoners were generally sent into exile and discriminated against in ways which affected them materially and psychologically.

NOTES

1 *Arkhipelag GULag*, Parts III–IV, YMCA, Paris (1974), p. 52.
2 *Ibid.*, p. 45.
3 *Ibid.*
4 A. Y. Vyshinskii, *Ot tyurem k vospitatelnym uchrezhdeniyam*, Moscow, Sovetskoe Zakonodatelstvo (1934).
5 I. L. Averbakh, in A. Y. Vyshinskii (ed.), *Ot prestupleniya k trudu*, Moscow, Sovetskoe Zakonodatelstvo (1936).
6 *Gulag Archipelago*, Parts III–IV, Collins/Harvill (1975), p. 104.
7 *Ibid.*, p. 109.
8 *Ibid.*, p. 121.
9 *Ibid.*, pp. 128 *et seq.*, 386–90.
10 *Ibid.*, p. 133.
11 *Ibid.*, p. 144; ref. P. Stuchka, *Guiding Principles of the Criminal Law*, Moscow (1919).
12 A. Y. Vyshinskii, *op. cit.*, quoted in *Gulag Archipelago*, Parts III–IV, *op. cit.*, p. 145.
13 *Gulag Archipelago, ibid.*, p. 147.
14 *Ibid.*
15 *Ibid.*, p. 204.

16 *Ibid.*
17 *Ibid.*, p. 256.
18 *Ibid.*
19 *Ibid.*, chapter 5 *passim*.
20 *Arkhipelag GULag*, Parts V–VII, YMCA, Paris (1976), pp. 415–26.
21 *Ibid.*, p. 468.
22 *Ibid.*, p. 470.
23 *Ibid.*, p. 473.
24 *Ibid.*, p. 474.
25 *Ibid.*, pp. 478–81.
26 *Ibid.*, p. 580.

5 *The Gulag Archipelago* (C) Soviet camps and their effect on Soviet society

Without dwelling on the wealth of detail about camp conditions supplied by Solzhenitsyn, I will concentrate on certain characteristics of the camps and the effect of the camps on Soviet society as a whole. A crucial characteristic of the Gulag Archipelago was that the authorities had unlimited power to send Soviet citizens there. Any limitations to the power of the 'dictatorship of the proletariat' would be viewed by Marxists as counter-revolutionary bourgeois pseudo-concepts. Moreover the authorities frequently flouted their own laws, for example concerning a two-week maximum term for defaulters in 'penalty isolators'.[1] The Soviet regime invented the soul-destroying technique of 'second term' for newly released prisoners.[2] All this confirms Solzhenitsyn's Actonian conviction that 'Unlimited power in the hands of limited people always leads to cruelty.'[3]

In addition to those corrupted by power at the top of the system, secondary groups, such as the stool-pigeons and trusties, camp guards and free workers (whose communities, which Solzhenitsyn calls 'Campside', were attached to the camps), all relied on the system and supported it.

Since the population of the Gulag Archipelago from the 1920s to 1953–6 was on average 8 per cent of the total,[4] its effect was like that of a huge tumour in the body of Soviet society. Solzhenitsyn says, 'Everything of the most infectious nature in the Archipelago . . . in human relations, morals, views, and language . . . dispersed through the entire country.'[5]

One special category of prisoners in the Archipelago was that of the thieves, the criminal elements as opposed to the majority of prisoners who were 'politicals'. Their own special code of coercion, theft, protection rackets and murder is fully discussed by Solzhenitsyn. The quintessence of their philosophy is summed up in the phrase, 'You today, me tomorrow.' And this variation on the theme of 'I'm all right Jack: the devil take the hindermost' was common in the camps as a means to survival. Solzhenitsyn says, 'The thieves' philosophy, which initially had conquered the Archipelago, easily swept further and captured the All-Union ideological market, a wasteland without any stronger ideology.'[6] Here it is strongly suggested that Marxism has little moral advice to, or influence over, the Soviet public. Similarly, camp attitudes towards conscientious work (minimise it in order to survive) are also transported to society at large. And many other effects are evident as well. Solzhenitsyn summarises them as follows:

(1) Constant fear (owing to lack of rights).
(2) Servitude (owing to being tied to one's place of residence, any protest is easily located and dealt with.)
(3) Secrecy and mistrust.
(4) Universal ignorance (owing to the 'atomisation of society' and state control of the press).
(5) Squealing and betrayal as a form of existence (encouraged from an early age).
(6) Corruption of individual integrity and the 'lie' as a form of existence. (Collaboration with the security police is approved, and there are penalties for not collaborating, but this involves one in spying and betrayal. The ideological 'line' must always be supported, often in a positive way, even if the individuals concerned do not believe it.)
(7) Cruelty.
(8) Slave psychology.

All of these accusations are fully argued and illustrated.[7] 'Thus it is', says Solzhenitsyn, 'that the Archipelago takes its vengeance on the Soviet Union for its creation.'[8]

The greatest single source of inefficiency in the economic sphere was the inflated work norms, which forced people to falsify their work reports in order to survive. The term used to describe this practice was *tukhta*, and Solzhenitsyn describes it as one of the pillars on which the Gulag Archipelago stands.[9]

Naturally, such a system tended to benefit the criminal rather than the honest man. Solzhenitsyn dwells on this theme at some length. In the first place, thieves were regarded by Stalin as 'socially friendly elements', because they were destructive of bourgeois property, as well as being depicted in Marxist theory as victims of their previous environment and responding to this environment in an adventurous way. Hence they received special privileges in the camps, shorter sentences and amnesties. Solzhenitsyn describes their power as great: 'They had unbridled power over the population of their own country [the Gulag Archipelago] . . . power they had never before had in history, never in any state in all the world. . . .'[10] The Stalin amnesty of 1945 was limited to those with three-year sentences, but no 'political' prisoner (incarcerated under article 58) received this kind of sentence.

So the amnesty applied only to the real criminals and also to deserters, while those who were captured by the Germans were retained as 'politicals'. This, surely, is a kind of topsy-turvy land, and Solzhenitsyn exclaims bitterly, 'And they want morality from the people!'[11] A good example of this topsy-turvydom was as follows. A certain Dr Zubov and his wife shielded and sheltered a deserter who was no relative of theirs: they just took pity on him. Later, under pressure, he turned them in for this, since he named them under interrogation. Their action was interpreted as anti-Soviet intent (article 58-10) and organisation, since they comprised husband and wife (article 58-11). In post-war years, all politicals received 25 years as we have seen above. But finally in 1962, their case was reviewed and they were found guilty instead of the correct offence, namely that of aiding a deserter (193-17-7g), for which the penalty was five years. So they finally qualified for the amnesty back-dated to 1945. The original charge had been pinned on them because the authorities could not believe that their action had been disinterested. Solzhenitsyn remarks, 'Now that's what the rancourous, vengeful, unreasonable law fears and what it does not fear!'[12] In response to the amnesty, for which incidentally Stalin derived no little international credit, a new slogan for display in the camps was coined: 'For the broadest amnesty we shall respond to our dear Party and government with doubled productivity!' The ones amnestied were the criminals, but the ones who responded with doubled productivity were the politicals.[13]

Among these 'politicals' were men of real talent. Solzhenitsyn mentions for example a fellow prisoner from his early days of arrest, one Gammerov, who although very weak and involved in hard labour in a clay pit, found the energy to compose poetry and discuss the philosophy of V. Soloviev with Solzhenitsyn. They sometimes compared their fate in that clay pit with young men of about their own age at Oxford or the Sorbonne, who still at that time supported the USSR. Gammerov, whose verses are now forgotten, died in that first winter. Solzhenitsyn comments bitterly,

> Only at some time in their old age, in the course of composing encyclopedias, would they [the former young men they had been discussing] notice with astonishment that they could not find any worthy Russian names for our letters – for all the letters of our alphabet.[14]

Of course, socialist theory provided for some cultural facilities in a number of the camps. A former head of Gulag, I. Apeter, is quoted in the work by Vyshinskii mentioned in the previous chapter, as saying

'To the prison construction of capitalist countries, the proletariat of the USSR counterposes its *cultural* construction.'[15] Camps had their own 'Cultural and Educational Section' (KVCh), whose chief had to be a free employee and from 'strata close to the proletariat'. Quite often, then, some young worker in his twenties without any tertiary education, who had himself been released from the 'productive process' would lecture professors on 'The role of labour in the process of correction'. They also had the function of 'reporting . . . the mood of the zeks' (i.e. they were stool-pigeons). They organised posters, campaigns, slogans, and such entertainments as choirs and amateur theatricals. The campaigns took the form of manipulation of prisoners in such processes as 'Comrades' Courts' and mass meetings for such aims as 'The struggle with the aid of the prisoners themselves against equalising wages' (i.e. some prisoners were encouraged to denounce others for not working hard enough). It was important, it seems, not to leave the prisoner too much to himself after work: hence loudspeakers and the camp press were very much in evidence. (It was claimed at times that the existence of a press in prison proved the existence of a free press.) Another activity was the use of 'suggestion' or complaints boxes of various kinds. These proved useful sources of information, as well as sometimes yielding ideas or inventions. The inventions which were taken up tended to be ones with military or prison/detection application. Meanwhile, Solzhenitsyn gives examples of scientists with more creative or less servile powers who perished on general work.[16]

The Cultural and Educational Sections provided some outlets for the artist, provided he was not too original in his paintings, but the facilities provided for talented people with less obviously marketable outputs were less good. Poets and musicians, composers, sculptors and prose writers were all disadvantaged. 'And yet at the same time', says Solzhenitsyn, 'the Archipelago provided a unique, exceptional, opportunity for our literature and perhaps . . . even for world literature.'[17] He develops this point in a fascinating footnote which says much about Solzhenitsyn's own social philosophy. He differentiates in any society between a ruling class or uppermost stratum, and a class of those ruled, or lower strata. This he sees as inevitable because of differing ability, educational opportunity, and money. The uppermost stratum he divides into two: one section has been preoccupied with its own (rather recherché) class, while the other section has written about both themselves and the lower strata. The lower strata have also tended to divide into two: those writing mainly about those above, often with either envy or servility, and those writing about themselves. In this category he places folklore of all kinds. Hitherto, especially in pre-revolutionary Russia, that group 'pondering the lower strata' tended to be blinded by their pity for them, and generally failed to empathise with them, but

Solzhenitsyn regards the type of literature pondering the lower strata as probably the most important, on account of its universality. Good examples of this include Cervantes and Dostoevskii. And Solzhenitsyn notes that slavery had transformed Cervantes, while hard labour had been the crucial turning point for Dostoevskii. The Gulag Archipelago, says Solzhenitsyn, must have provided this essential training ground for many Russian writers, but 'the bearers of this merged experience perished'.[18]

Few would dispute however that among the survivors, Solzhenitsyn himself is one representative of those who have created a great Russian and world literature. He claims that his experiences in prison and exile were largely responsible for the personal and spiritual transformation which enabled this contribution to be made. He even goes as far as to say, 'Bless you prison, for having been in my life!'[19] Yet he does make some distinction between prison and the hard-labour camps, and acknowledges that his comments can be of little application to those dead or bereaved. Nevertheless, he does have this to say: 'Whenever I recall or encounter a former zek [from the camps] I encounter a real personality.'[20] The word in Russian is *lichnost'*, which in my view carries a different connotation from the English word 'personality'. *Lichnost'* implies a well-formed, developed, full character. And while the camps had a damaging effect on many people, corrupting the majority of its inmates as we have seen, Solzhenitsyn believes that camp experience did not corrupt those with a stable nucleus to their personality, but rather helped them to develop. He gives examples of people, many of whom were Christians, who by their steadfastness and courage, their determination not to collaborate, their inner tenacity to life which enabled them to survive, resisted both the authorities and the endemic corruption of camp life. Solzhenitsyn argues that it is these people who show us how to resist the creators of the Gulag Archipelago, whereas the various genuine 'politicals' such as the loyalists or the Trotskyites proved to be either laughable or futile.[21]

In Parts V–VII of the *Gulag Archipelago*, Solzhenitsyn records many risings and attempted risings in camps. He notes forms of protest including demonstration, hunger strikes, escapes and revolts. Few were successful in any way at all, he says, because there was seldom the necessary unity of action and the population were afraid to help fugitives, unlike those of Tsarist times.[22] Some of the national groupings attempted to form politically active associations, but they were easy prey for the authorities and found it difficult to recruit members.[23] The penalties for attempted escape became extremely severe after the war, carrying a twenty-year sentence.[24] Sometimes guards would kill prisoners if they were thought to be attempting an escape. Solzhenitsyn also notes several camp uprisings, including the one at Ekibastuz on

19 January 1951,[25] and a serious strike and demonstration among ordinary workers at Novocherkassk on 2 June 1962, when 70–80 workers were shot down for demonstrating against price rises of butter and meat (the local students were locked in their quarters).[26]

Solzhenitsyn is saying, then, that the normal channels of political activity are strongly, and usually effectively, blocked by the authorities, and that new means of moral protest are required. This view has profound implications for the politics of Solzhenitsyn.

SUMMARY

A camp system based on the unlimited power of the state and its officials created certain groups which had a stake in the continuation of that system. These included secret police, camp guards, stool-pigeons and informers, and free workers and their attendant communities. The total number of people involved, including the prisoners, was a large percentage of the population and the manners and customs of this percentage have infected the whole of Soviet society. These characteristics of camp life include: fear; servitude; ignorance; betrayal as a form of existence; lack of integrity; cruelty; slave psychology. There is also a universal tendency to falsify work reports, which results in economic inefficiency.

Such a system benefited the criminal rather than the honest man, whereas the really honest and talented were discriminated against. The progressive-sounding 'Cultural and Educational Sections' in the camps were used by the authorities for their own propaganda purposes, for gathering information, and for cheap entertainment; but they benefited very few creative artists apart from some painters. Indeed Solzhenitsyn believes that the camp system destroyed a whole national literature, which, because of the conditions of its birth, would have been a significant contribution to world literature.

Nevertheless the experience of the camps did have some beneficial effects on the development of certain individuals, and Solzhenitsyn believes that these people, a kind of spiritual elite, hold the key to national revival, rather than those who seek to protest politically in more conventional ways.

NOTES
1 *Gulag Archipelago*, Parts III–IV, Collins/Harvill (1975), p. 415.
2 *Ibid.*, p. 375.
3 *Ibid.*, p. 546.
4 *Ibid.*, p. 632.
5 *Ibid.*, p. 564.
6 *Ibid.*, pp. 564–5.

7   *Ibid.*, pp. 632–53.
8   *Ibid.*, p. 565.
9   *Ibid.*, p. 161.
10 *Ibid.*, p. 435.
11 *Ibid.*, p. 188.
12 *Ibid.*, p. 190.
13 *Ibid.*
14 *Ibid.*, p. 196.
15 A. Y. Vyshinskii, *Ot tyurem k vospitatelnym uchrezhdeniyam*, Moscow, Sovetskoe Zakonodatelstvo (1934), p. 43.
16 *Gulag Archipelago*, Parts III–IV, *op. cit.*, p. 483.
17 *Ibid.*, pp. 489–90.
18 *Ibid.*, p. 491.
19 *Ibid.*, p. 617.
20 *Ibid.*, p. 623.
21 *Vide*, for example, *ibid*, pp. 336, 390.
22 *Arkhipelag GULag*, Parts V–VII, YMCA, Paris (1976), pp. 100–5.
23 *Ibid.*, pp. 251–2.
24 *Ibid.*, p. 399.
25 *Ibid.*, pp. 73–5.
26 *Ibid.*, pp. 557–64.

6 Soviet society as distorter of reality and the individual

Solzhenitsyn's claims for basic rights of the individual before the law and the penal system, and his insistence on the rule of law, both as regards the actions of individuals and the state itself, suggest a connection with the traditions of liberalism. However, Solzhenitsyn may be termed a liberal, only in a certain basic sense: he is saying more than this, partially perhaps because the Soviet state has made demands on its population unparalleled in history at least up to the mid-twentieth century.

Apart from virtually eliminating the concept of legality, it has also claimed a monopoly of truth, and each man's perception of certain aspects of reality, such as the past. In *One Day in the Life of Ivan Denisovich* Solzhenitsyn suggests, impressionistically, that the state has become almost more powerful than nature: the camp searchlights, we are told, 'outshone the stars'.[1] When Shukhov argues with Buinovskii, that 'every greybeard knows that the sun stands highest at dinner time,' Buinovskii answers, 'a new decree has been passed, and now the sun stands highest at One.' ('Mean to say even the sun in the heavens must kowtow to their decrees?')[2]

The state, as personified by Stalin, also demands total personal subservience to its (his) whims and decisions. This requires abandonment of personally formulated conclusions, as experienced by Zotov in *Incident at Krechetovka Station*, when he begins to have doubts about the strategic conduct of the war and the possibility of defeat. '[This] was blasphemy, it was an insult to the omniscient, omnipotent Father and Teacher, who was always there, who foresaw everything. . . .'[3]

Monopoly of information and rectitude is moreover reinforced by the state control of the mass media and, to a certain extent too, of official vocabulary. As Zotov records, 'From the official news bulletins it was impossible to discover where the front line ran; it was not even clear who held Kaluga or who held Kharkov.'[4] This monopoly was so embracing that Zotov and his friend Paulina (in the local post office) 'would leaf nervously through the papers looking for any crumbs of information that might explain the course of the War'.[5] This state of affairs is perhaps understandable in wartime, as Zotov admits when the actor Tveritinov says it is dangerous to ask questions 'these days'. Tveritinov counters, 'It was the same before the War.' Zotov, a totally dedicated party member, asserts that he 'didn't notice', but Tveritinov insists that a significant change occurred after 1937.[6]

Questions, discussion and even private thought become dangerous, as Zotov himself admits. 'Zotov never spoke his thoughts aloud – to do so would be dangerous – but he was afraid even to say them to himself.'[7] Moreover, the monopoly of thought and language is made more pervasive, in Solzhenitsyn's view, by the quality of the language used. For Solzhenitsyn, the quality and beauty of language is a measure of humanity, and he is appalled by the crude language which permeated the official Russian language under the influence of the Stalin era. As Nerzhin says in *The First Circle*, 'Lenin was to the point, so full of feeling and so precise, and then I come to this mush. Everything Stalin says is crude and stupid – he always misses the most important point.'[8] This crudeness permeats into all areas of life; even place-names are affected. In *Matryona's Home*, the narrator comments on the name of the local township: '*Peatproduce?* If only Turgenev were alive today to see what violence is being done to the Russian language.'[9]

Reality and individual relationships are also much distorted by the prevailing atmosphere of paranoia and mistrust. For example, Rusanov in *Cancer Ward* sees all the doctors and nurses in the hospital as sinister, at least on first admission to the ward. He muses, 'Assassins in white coats – that was well said.'[10] (N.B. This rather explicit reference to the 'Doctors' plot' does not occur in the 'Possev' text.) Similarly, in *Incident at Krechetovka Station*, a story whose main theme is in one sense simply paranoid delusion, Zotov is unreasonably suspicious of the stranger Tveritinov simply because he is travelling by himself. He refuses to let a railway official (Dygin) reveal the nature of his train's cargo in front of Tveritinov: Zotov's absurd reasoning is that if Tveritinov is a spy, he could destroy the load, which consisted of 20,000 trenching tools, and since in certain circumstances a soldier without a spade could lose his life, then destruction of 20,000 spades is equivalent to destroying 20,000 soldiers' lives.

Finally, after a long conversation in which Zotov 'lowers his guard', it is the failure of Tveritinov to recognise the name 'Stalingrad' which causes his downfall. Tveritinov asks Zotov to repeat the name; 'What was it called before?'* 'Something in Zotov snapped and he suddenly froze. Was it possible? A Soviet citizen and didn't know Stalingrad?'[11] The ensuing arrest of Tveritinov is followed by remorse on the part of Zotov, but he knows that it would be dangerous to show too much

* Tsaritsyn.

interest in the case. He asks the NKVD officer to whom Tveritinov had been sent, ' "Do you remember a man called Tveritinov?" . . . "Why do you ask?" The Security Officer frowned significantly.'[12]

Mistrust and paranoia, potent weapons in the hands of a dictator bent on the 'atomisation' of society, eventually create a situation where no-one feels able to trust his own judgement of others more than a little way. For example, when the young MVD supervisors are about to take up their posts at the Mavrino camp in *The First Circle*, it has to be explained to them that the prisoners really have been guilty of the most appalling crimes, such as treason, but 'they did not openly bare their fangs, but always bore a mask of courtesy and good breeding'.[13] Moreover, even between the prisoners themselves, there is little mutual trust, partly because of the system of informers, such as Siromakha in *The First Circle*, undetected by any of the main characters until it is too late; and partly because of the extreme hardship of the conditions. For example, Shukhov had 'hidden his trowel in a nearby cranny. Although he was among his own lads, one of them might swap it for his own.'[14] Similarly, private conversations between prisoners or patients can sometimes give rise to suspicion in a society which claims a monopoly of ideological truth. Kostoglotov is an immediate suspect as far as Rusanov is concerned (Rusanov is the odious security man depicted in *Cancer Ward*) because Kostoglotov attacks a government institution in public. (The institution was in fact the 'government'* synod which had excommunicated Tolstoy.) Rusanov had not heard the exact name of the official body concerned, but 'what he had to do now was to stop the argument tactfully and *check up* on Kostoglotov at the first opportunity'.[15]

In such a situation, only a few people can have any inkling of what is going on: those (in particular party members) who can read the 'esoteric signals' given out by the official press. (This term has been used in reference to the Soviet press by Myron Rush.) For example, in the cancer ward, there is some dispute between Rusanov and Kostoglotov about who should have first glance at the morning paper. Rusanov muses, 'No-one here could possibly understand a newspaper as he [Rusanov] did. He regarded newspapers as a widely distributed instruction written in fact in code. . . .'[16] Even this glimpse of reality is limited and partial, for the guidance of party officials so that they may be able to carry out their functions more effectively and perspicaciously. This practice also applies to official publications such as the party history.

Distortion of reality by the state is seen by Solzhenitsyn as a fearful crime, as also is the practice of perverting people's view of the world,

* The Russian words for 'government' and 'orthodox' have some similarities.

of persuading them that reality is not what it may seem to the untutored eye. This abhorrence held by Solzhenitsyn is, I think, indicated by his protests about the use of coercive psychiatric hospitals* for those whose 'perception' of Soviet society is deviant from the official point of view. Referring to the incarceration of Zhores Medvedev, Solzhenitsyn has stated,

> the incarceration of free-thinking healthy people in mad-houses is *spiritual murder*, it is a variation of the *gas chamber*, but it is even more cruel; the torture of people being killed is more malicious and more prolonged.[17]

Distortion of reality and individuals by the state goes hand in hand with considerable inefficiency and neglect of people's real and basic needs. While the state claims the rights of totalitarian surveillance, and total allegiance from the people, it does not adequately fulfil its duties with respect to those people. For example, in *The First Circle*, anyone intending to travel a long distance by train 'had to furnish documents proving that he had official grounds for being a burden on public transport'.[18] The social services, too, come in for some severe criticism: in the short story, *The Right Hand*, the hospital refuses to admit Bobrov, who is apparently a terminal case, because, as the receptionist says, 'Don't you know the routine? We only admit patients at nine a.m.!'[19] Bobrov, a veteran of the Civil War, should have been in receipt of a special pension, but for some reason failed to qualify. So also Matryona (in the short story *Matryona's Home*) had interminable difficulties:

> She was sick, but she was not certified as disabled; she had worked on the collective farm for a quarter of a century, yet because she had not been directly engaged on production she was not entitled to a personal pension.[20]

This lack of attention to individual needs, and the subordination of people to the abstract workings of rules, sometimes leads to extreme hardship. The officer Dygin in *Incident at Krechetovka Station* has a troop of reservists under his command who have not eaten for eleven days, because they had the misfortune to arrive at stations en route after the stores had closed. And it was 'the rule at every ration store that no rations were ever issued in arrears'.[21]

Moreover, a possibly connected characteristic is that the state is apparently unable or unwilling to change its basic methods or even (since 1953) its personnel. This '*immobilisme*' is naturally welcomed by such people as Rusanov, who comments, 'and whichever way the

---

* For comment on Soviet practice in this respect, see *New Scientist* (2 November 1972).

[economic] reorganisation went, whether this way or that, no-one, including Pavel Nikolaievich [Rusanov], ever suffered a drop in rank. There were only promotions.'[22] One may perhaps assume that during the period of the Great Terror, people in the state and party apparatus may have tended to show little enthusiasm for criticism or reform, even if, as Inkeles and Bauer have shown,[23] the degree of 'social mobility' was greater.

The distortion of individuals by the state, and the lack of attention to individual needs and desires in the name, presumably, of some notion of providing for the 'collective' has its effect, says Solzhenitsyn, on the younger generation. For example, in an effort to keep up the 'success rate' of the local school, pupils are sometimes moved up whether or not their work has merited this. Hence one of the teacher Ignatich's pupils at Tal'novo (*Matryona's Home*) draws the conclusion that he does not need to do any homework.[24] Perhaps more seriously, this lack of attention to individual needs tends to produce a kind of equal and opposite reaction in the form of indifference and hostility to the 'system' on the part of the pupils. A teacher at the Technical Institute, which is the *mise-en-scène* for the novel *For the Good of the Cause*, records that when he spoke at a guest lecture, no-one bothered to listen to him – 'they just did whatever they felt like'. And he goes on to say, 'For some reason, the sight of them frightens me slightly. . . .'[25] The younger generation, says Solzhenitsyn, has a tendency to be materialistic, brutal and insensitive. However, this is partly because the older generation is insensitive to their needs. As Grachikov says in *For the Good of the Cause*, if the authorities take away the new school building, 'they'll never forget we've cheated them. If you cheat people once, then they realise that you may cheat them again.'[26] Solzhenitsyn goes further along this line of thought to argue that the state may be creating a generation which will eventually threaten Soviet society. By teaching young people that it is socially acceptable to inform on their elders or to engage in mob violence against, for example, religious groups, the state may be creating an inhuman generation which it cannot adequately control. At the end of the *Easter Procession* he sounds a warning: 'What good can we expect of our future generations? The truth is that one day they will turn and trample on us all. And as for those who urged them on to this, they will trample on them too.'[27] It may be said, perhaps, that Solzhenitsyn is claiming some very high standards as a minimum of reasonable behaviour, and strongly objects to any kind of petty vandalism on the part of youth. Hence in the short story *Zakhar Kalita*, Solzhenitsyn deprecates the carving of names on the battle monument. It should be noted that Solzhenitsyn has extremely high personal standards and adopts a strongly moralistic tone which borders at times upon the obsessional and the absolute. In this he resembles

c

Tolstoi, with perhaps more than a hint of taking the sins of the world upon his shoulders. Solzhenitsyn's love for humanity is modified by his hatred of what is inhuman in man.

A social system which has a degrading effect on its citizens naturally attracts people into administration who are themselves degraded. At the top, such people as Abakumov (or Yezhov?) are apt to be successful, and in the prisons, informers like Siromakha (*The First Circle*) and professional crooks like Goldtooth and Georgie (*The Love-Girl and the Innocent*) flourish. No less a commentator than Bukharin himself has corroborated this process, when he commented to Nicolaevskii on 'the real dehumanisation of the people working in the Soviet apparatus' (in 1930–1).[28] By the same token, a large number of the most outstanding people in society are in prison, including such as Professor Chelnov in *The First Circle*, loyal communists such as Rubin, and the innocent and the ignorant such as Spiridon.

However, for Solzhenitsyn himself, the total effect of the camps has been to strengthen him in his perception of truths, both great and small. As Alex in the play *Candle in the Wind* says, 'I had ten years of long and careful reflection behind me and already I know the truth of the saying that the true savour of life is not to be gained from big things but from little ones.'[29] Gleb Nerzhin in *The First Circle* makes some bigger claims about the influences of his experiences when he says to Sologdin, 'what I've been through, and seen others go through, should give me a good idea of what history is about – don't you think so?'[30] Some of Solzhenitsyn's passages have a quality of writing which may be compared to the Dialogues of Plato – for example, the conversation between Kostoglotov and Shulubin in *Cancer Ward*;[31] and for this reason one is reminded of Plato's philosopher king, who has experienced the truth but is baffled by the majority of his fellows who still regard the insubstantial shadows of official Soviet life as the reality. At the same time, Solzhenitsyn is sure that the truth of the Stalin era will eventually be told, and that justice, so far as this will still be possible, will be done. Stalin's heirs and those who carried out his orders must surely be stricken, from time to time, with guilt and remorse, or at least with fear (Solzhenitsyn sees admission of guilt as the crucial factor). In *Cancer Ward*, Rusanov dreams during the course of his apparently fatal illness about the people he has caused to be imprisoned or 'purged'; and these memories haunt his conscience. But perhaps more frightening to him is the news that one of his victims, unjustly denounced in the Purges, has been rehabilitated. When his wife Kapitolina tells Rusanov this startling information, 'she missed the moment when Pasher turned whiter than the sheets of his bed'.[32]

SUMMARY

In this chapter, I have shown that Solzhenitsyn depicts the Soviet experience as responsible for: suppression of individual rights and freedom of thought (including the degradation of the Russian language); creation of mutual mistrust and paranoia; attempted distortion of the public's perception of reality and history; creation of an atmosphere conducive to widespread cruelty and indifference in people's mutual relations, the social services, and among the young; economic inefficiency; the promotion of criminals and the suppression of the innocent and the talented; and finally the paradoxically beneficial effects of the camps on some individuals which may enable the truth eventually to be told.

NOTES
1   *Sobranie Sochinenii*, Vol. 1, p. 9.
2   *Ibid.*, pp. 50–1.
3   *Ibid.*, pp. 138–9.
4   *Ibid.*, p. 138.
5   *Ibid.*, p. 155.
6   *Ibid.*, p. 174.
7   *Ibid.*, p. 139.
8   *Sob. Soch.*, Vol. 3, p. 53.
9   *Sob. Soch.*, Vol. 2, p. 68.
10 *Ibid.*
11 *Ibid.*, p. 186. The Russian text is 'I-vsyo oborvalos' i okholnulo v Zotove.' In other words, there is a sudden *total* realisation, a shade of meaning not available in English.
12 *Sob. Soch.*, Vol. 1, p. 193.
13 *Sob. Soch.*, Vol. 3, p. 38.
14 *Sob. Soch.*, Vol. 1, p. 46.
15 *Sob. Soch*, Vol. 2, p. 158.
16 *Ibid.*, p. 236.
17 *Chronicle of Current Events*, No. 14 (30 June 1970).
18 *Sob. Soch.*, Vol. 3, p. 289.
19 *Sob. Soch.*, Vol. 5, p. 217.
20 *Sob. Soch.*, Vol. 1, p. 203.
21 *Ibid.*, p. 192.
22 *Sob. Soch.*, Vol. 2, p. 23.
23 A. Inkeles and R. Bauer, *The Soviet Citizen*, Havard University Press, Cambridge, Mass. (1959).
24 *Sob. Soch.*, Vol. 2, p. 212.
25 *Sob. Soch.*, Vol. 1, p. 238.
26 *Ibid.*, p. 283.
27 *Sob. Soch.*, Vol. 5, p. 237.
28 B. Nikolaevskii, *Power and the Soviet Elite*, Pall Mall Press (1966), pp. 18–19.
29 *Sob. Soch.*, Vol. 5, p. 210.
30 *Sob. Soch.*, Vol. 3, p. 193.
31 *Sob. Soch.*, Vol. 2, chapter 31.
32 *Ibid.*, p. 209. ('Pasha stal belee bel'ya' – 'Pasha became whiter than white'.)

7 The nature of the individual and the rights of humans

Aleksandr Solzhenitsyn is Russia's greatest living writer, concerned above all with the destiny of his own country. Before his compulsory exile abroad, he himself said, 'For my entire life, I have had the soil of my homeland under my feet; only *its* pain do I hear, only about it do I write.'[1] Solzhenitsyn's work is also a contribution of great importance to world literature. And it seems that for many years Solzhenitsyn tried to work within the confines of the regime, adjusting his proposed publications to both censorship and the capacity of public opinion to read the truth. How is it, then, that such a man could be driven into exile, into a political position of unyielding opposition to the Soviet regime? Only an inflexible regime, mortally afraid of great literature, freedom of thought and the exposure of its own past, could have achieved this result.

In this chapter I am concerned with an exploration of Solzhenitsyn's ideas about the rights of individuals as members of the Soviet national community. He derives these ideas from his fundamental beliefs about the nature of individuals as members of the human race.

In the first place, Solzhenitsyn sees the individual *conscience* as an infallible guide to justice. I quote here Solzhenitsyn's views *in extenso* because these, it seems to me, are the foundation stone of his philosophy of man. This is not so much a 'faith' as a personal conviction arrived at from experience, both of his own reactions to injustice and of the reactions of others. As he had rejected the 'official' morality and its world-outlook (a rejection which, I have argued, was a long drawn-out process, not lightly arrived at), his long years in prison may be seen in one sense as a search for a new foundation for his philosophy of man in society, for his political thought. This philosophy is referred to in *Cancer Ward* as 'ethical socialism' although, as I hope to show, it cannot really be classed as socialism in any sense.

Solzhenitsyn's philosophy is based on a belief in the 'objective' existence of justice, and our ability to perceive it, if we so desire, through the operation of conscience. In his *Advice to Three Students*, Solzhenitsyn reasons as follows:

Justice has been the common patrimony of humanity throughout the ages . . . obviously it is a concept which is inherent in man, since it cannot be traced to any other source. . . . There is nothing relative about justice, as there is nothing relative about conscience. . . . As our intelligence is not sufficient to grasp, to understand and to foresee the course of history . . . you will never err if you act in any social situation in accordance with justice. . . . Convictions based on conscience are as infallible as the internal rhythm of the heart. . . .[2]

Solzhenitsyn goes on to claim that the dictates of conscience are in fact *absolute*. As Nemov says in *The Love-Girl and the Innocent*, 'you know something – sometimes I think to myself, are our lives so important? Are they the most valuable thing we have?' Lyuba, the heroine to whom he is speaking, replies with the query, 'What else is there?', and Nemov replies, 'maybe . . . conscience . . .'.[3] Solzhenitsyn is obviously profoundly impressed by the number of people he has met in prison who have flouted what one of the leading characters in *The First Circle* (Yakonov) calls the 'universal law of "charity begins at home" '[4] – that is to say, such people as Nerzhin and Gerasimovich in *The First Circle* who eventually choose an almost certain transfer away from the comforts of a 'special' prison (the 'first circle' of Mavrino) to the Northern labour camps, rather than cooperate with the authorities of 'State Security'. This apparently irrational behaviour, justified in such apparently insubstantial terms as Nerzhin's 'but if you die knowing that you are not a swine, that's something, isn't it?',[5] serves as the basis for Solzhenitsyn's beliefs. He clearly rejects the official Marxist view that 'Being determines consciousness', arguing that the individual consciousness is, or can be, an active 'eternal' force. For example, the love for one person, such as Nerzhin's wife Nadya, as a unique individual of ultimate value in herself, can last through the years of separation in prison, despite the terrible restrictions imposed by society and general opinion, or the temptations presented in the person of girls like Simochka.

Man, says Solzhenitsyn, has a conscience, and a consciousness aware of its free will: this is a natural condition of mankind, but not, perhaps, of animals. As Spiridon's wise aphorism puts it, 'the wolf hounds are right and the cannibals are wrong'.[6] The unique quality of man, when compared with the unreflective instinctual behaviour of animals, suggests that he has some kind of special value in the scheme of created nature; a special individuality and purpose. Solzhenitsyn identifies this unique quality of man with the possession of a *soul*, which cannot therefore be controlled by the authorities without consent. As Shukhov says to himself as he is being searched, 'come on, paw me as hard as you like. There's nothing but my soul in my chest.'[7] Solzhenitsyn also implies that this soul cannot always be controlled by any state coercive apparatus, especially if people are aware of their own 'spiritual' quality. Shulubin in *Cancer Ward* has some comments to make about this: 'Sometimes I feel quite distinctly that what is inside me is not all of me. There's something else, sublime, quite indestructible, some tiny fragment of the universal spirit.'[8] Solzhenitsyn goes on to put forward a view comparable with the neo-Platonism of Wordsworth in 'Intimations of Immortality . . .' when he states (also in *Cancer Ward*): 'The meaning of existence was to preserve untarnished, undisturbed, and undistorted, the image of eternity which each person is born with – as far as possible.'[9]

Quite naturally, therefore, Solzhenitsyn's political beliefs are based on a primary concern for the rights of the individual. For example, people have the right to make their own moral choices, as Kostoglotov insists to the hospital authorities in *Cancer Ward* when he protests that his decisions are being made for him by others. 'And once again I become a grain of sand, just like I was in the camp. Once again, nothing depends on me.'[10] An allied point is made by the character Khorobrov in *The First Circle* who is 'firm in the belief that freedom starts with respect for other people's rights'.[11] In the case of Khorobrov, this statement applied only to the relatively trivial example that some people object to others smoking in a confined space; however, Solzhenitsyn extends such principles to a sophisticated demand for civil liberties.[12] Innokenti Volodin discovers this point of view expressed in his mother's writings (*The First Circle*), along with the politically important rejection of all notions of 'official ideology', or any 'science' of society as interpreted by the party: 'Just as the essence of food cannot be expressed in calories, so the essence of life is not to be conveyed by any formula, however brilliant.'[13] Solzhenitsyn rejects the idea of an all-embracing philosophy or ideology of society, and for similar reasons, he is also scathing about the necessity for 'official' literature. In the first place, this is a denial of man's basic inhumanity: 'man has distinguished himself from the animal world by *thought* and *speech*. And these, naturally, should be *free*. If they are put in chains, we will return to the state of the animals.'[14] Solzhenitsyn also points out that the concept of official literature also tends to kill literature itself. For example, he states this explicitly in his Open Letter to the Fourth Writers' Congress (16 May 1967),[15] and this point of view is perhaps somewhat substantiated by the fact that officially approved literature does not sell very readily. As the students in *For the Good of the Cause* notice, 'There are so many of those novels turning yellow in the windows, and all the shelves are packed with them. You go in a year later, and they're all still there.'[16] Such a policy tends to attract large numbers of mediocre writers who are all virtually indistinguishable from one another. For example, Dyoma in *Cancer Ward* is reading a book which was

> by A. Kozhevnikov, but there were also an S. Kozhevnikov and a V. Kozhevnikov. Dyoma was rather frightened at the thought of how many writers there were. In the previous century there had been about ten, all of them great; in this one there were thousands; change one letter and you had another writer. There was Safronov, and now there was Safonov – more than one, apparently. . . .[17]

In protesting about his eventual expulsion from the Writers' Union, Solzhenitsyn's opposition to the Marxist concept of 'class enemies' is once more very clear:

> In this way a sense of our common humanity is lost and its doom is accelerated. Should the Arctic ice melt tomorrow, we would all become a sea of drowning humanity, and into whose heads would you then be drilling your concepts of 'class struggle'? Not to mention the time when the few surviving bipeds will be wandering over the radioactive earth, dying.[18]

It is hardly surprising, perhaps, that Soviet Marxist–Leninists have attacked Solzhenitsyn's views as anathema. For example, one Novichenko stated at the Union of Writers Secretariat meeting of 22 September 1967, 'The ideological and political sense of "ethical socialism" is the negation of Marxism–Leninism.'[19]

Along with Solzhenitsyn's opposition to the official ideology and literature, and his opposition to the tenets of Marxism–Leninism, there goes a perceptible nostalgia for the archaic and the claim that certain aspects of modern life are inhuman. In the prose poem 'Freedom to breathe', Solzhenitsyn comments on the healing influence of the fragrance of his garden after rain, in contrast to the environment of modern technology. 'I cease to hear the motorcycles backfiring, the radios whining, the burble of loudspeakers. As long as there is fresh air to breathe under an apple tree after a shower, we may survive a little longer.'[20] Solzhenitsyn criticises the pace and speed of modern life: As the hospital doctors in *Cancer Ward* complain with reason, 'Everybody is always in a hurry! Whole lives to be decided in a single minute!'[21] In addition to all this, it seems that Solzhenitsyn does not regard urban life as an environment which enriches human life, as Marx would have believed (richer, that is, than the 'idiocy of rural life'); instead it is seen as a *distraction*, as the Prosecutor's daughter Clara (in *The First Circle*) discovers on returning to Moscow from her wartime evacuation: 'It was strange, but amid the bright lights the noise and traffic, it was as though all her thoughts about life, which had been so clear during the days of her illness, had become muddled and faded away.'[22]

Solzhenitsyn believes that modern man is in danger of losing his contacts with nature, which seem to him the source of health, both mental and physical. He has for example a deep scepticism about certain modern medical techniques and, like Kostoglotov, he opposes the idea of drugs as the way to *create* health. 'Why this twentieth-century gimmick? Why should every medicine be given by injection? You don't see anything similar in nature or among animals, do you?'[23] His argument seems to be along the lines of criticising man's narrow understanding of the workings of nature, and his limited and abstract thought capacity: Any medicine, such as hormone injections for patients like Kostoglotov, given in order to suppress the formation of secondary cancerous growth, has side-effects which the human researcher cannot foresee. Similarly, X-ray treatment for cancer in excessive doses is in itself carcinogenic. Man has overestimated his intelligence and has been carried away by his success in some areas of technology; but as Solzhenitsyn points out, in his prose poem 'The Duckling', 'with all our atomic might we shall never – never! – be able to make this feeble speck of yellow a duckling in a test tube.'[24] Man is merely a part of created nature – perhaps rather a special part, it is true – but he should be 'in tune' with its component fauna and flora. For example, kindness to animals is desirable, and we are told that in Matryona's life (*Matryona's Home*) even the plants in her living room, 'silent yet alive . . . filled the loneliness of Matryona's existence'.[25]

Individuals like Matryona, and the Kadmins in *Cancer Ward*, who realise these connections with nature, often seem a little old-fashioned. Matryona, we are told, 'obviously liked the idea of being photographed working at the old craft [weaving on a hand-loom]'.[26] The Kadmins in exile in Kazakhstan managed to obtain a round dining table and then to construct an archaic paraffin lamp which 'transformed the little clay hovel into a luxurious drawing-room of two centuries ago'.[27]

The implication of Solzhenitsyn's views would appear to be that modern technology can be a dehumanising influence, in that it is conducive to loss of contact with nature, loss of individualism, and perhaps also to over-centralised government, the imposition of official ideology and other aspects of modern life which he criticises, such as its speed and lack of provision for 'small-scale' human needs. In this sense, Solzhenitsyn might be thought to be unrealistic or even reactionary. However, I think that it might be more correct to see his philosophy, not as a romantic escapism, but rather as a reaction against an extremist regime, which still tries to eradicate or distort much of the past by falsifying history, which laid excessive stress on a crash programme of industrialisation, imposing misery on a great part of the countryside in the process, and which claimed to be solving substantial socio-economic problems in the name of the people as a whole when in fact it became an instrument of tyranny for one man with the individuals and peoples of the USSR as impotent pawns, manoeuvred this way and that in the execution of Stalin's purposes.

Solzhenitsyn's views about modern technology and economics have been made much more explicit since the publication of his 'Open Letter to Soviet Leaders' which appeared first in early 1974. In an introduction to this letter, the *Sunday Times* (3 March 1974) writes '[Solzhenitsyn] deplores the mindless policy of economic growth which has despoiled the beauty of Russia's cities and ruined the tranquillity of her countryside.' As Solzhenitsyn's political philosophy becomes more explicit and defined, it seems that he is beginning to enunciate ideas which, although derived from personal and specifically Russian experience, seem strangely relevant to the whole of the developed world. I shall deal with the 'Open Letter' at greater length in chapter 11.

In what sense, however (if at all), can Solzhenitsyn's views be termed 'socialist'? In one way, this can be seen as no more than a statement that man is a social animal, and that he should be actively aware of the life of the whole community, eschewing private happiness if it is bought at the expense of others and of turning a blind eye to their sufferings (as, for example, the State Prosecutor Makarygin does in his privileged environment depicted in *The First Circle*). It would be incorrect, in my opinion, to name Solzhenitsyn's beliefs as 'socialist' in any modern sense of the word: for Solzhenitsyn, it is relationships between individuals which matter most, and these it seems are not in any way dependent on a particular form of economic organisation, or property or production relationships. Good human relations can occur in any surroundings, such as Ivan Denisovich's camp, or the special prison at Mavrino, where Solzhenitsyn once again speaks in Platonic terms, referring to

a spirit of manly friendship and philosophy [which] hovered over the sail-shaped vault of the ceiling. Was this, perhaps, that state of bliss which all the philosophers of antiquity tried in vain to define and describe?[28]

Ultimately, this spirit of comradeship is based on awareness of common mortality. 'They all had the same enemy, death. What can divide human beings on earth once they are all faced with death?'[29] At the same time, Solzhenitsyn is realistic in that he does not prescribe the kind of high-level philosophical friendships encountered among the prisoners of Mavrino as a general norm. He regards ordinary, unheroic family life as the basis of most people's humanity and socialisation, and talks for example in *The First Circle* of 'that dogged wifely concern, that instinct which makes family life what it is and which keeps the human race going.'[30] Unlike the early Russian socialists,

Solzhenitsyn does not harbour illusions about the hidden wisdom or 'special' value of the common people:

> It was only character that mattered, and this was something that everybody had to forge for himself, by constant effort over the years. Only thus could one make oneself into a human being and hence be regarded as a tiny part of one's People.[31]

It might be thought that Solzhenitsyn has an identifiable special affection for the 'narod',* but it should be stressed that his portraits of such people as Spiridon, Matryona and Zakhar Kalita are all sketches of *individuals*, although perhaps in some sense universalised, as Matryona, who is 'that one righteous person without whom, as the saying goes, no city can stand. Nor the world.'[32] There is as far as I can see only one example of some figure or symbol of the Russian people as a whole in Solzhenitsyn's writings, and he is not so much a symbol of wisdom, the source of some peasant philosophy, but rather a symbol of resistance and survival: the survival of the Russian people under the yoke of Stalin, the Great Patriotic war, and other misfortunes. This occurs towards the end of *One Day*, where we are told that

> [the prisoner] had lost all his teeth and chewed his bread with iron gums. All life had drained out of his face, but it had been left, not sickly and feeble, but hard and dark like carved stone. And by his hands, big and cracked and blackened, you could see he'd had little opportunity of doing cushy jobs. (But he wasn't going to give in, oh no!)[33]

Solzhenitsyn is concerned above all with *individual* men and women, and insists that individuals must once again provide the yardstick for measuring what the government and its political economy can and cannot do. Hence also, government should be, as far as possible, government by *consent*. This is, in fact, an efficient method of management, as Grachikov in the novella *For the Good of the Cause* discovers.

> It was against [Grachikov's] nature to end conversations and meetings by giving orders; he tried to convince his opponents to the bitter end, so that they would admit, 'yes, you're right,' or else prove to him that he was wrong.[34]

This is not simply a desirable principle of government for Solzhenitsyn, it is also a desirable *style*. He is very keen to see changes in the Stalinist 'hard' line of administration, so aptly represented by Rusanov in

---

* 'Narod' means 'the People' in Russian, carrying a highly emotional collective connotation.

Cancer Ward or by the obkom* secretary Knorozov in *For the Good of the Cause*. As Knorozov says on one occasion to Grachikov, 'You're too soft, you don't act in the Soviet Way.' But Grachikov, we are told, 'stood his ground'. 'Why do you say that? Quite the contrary, I work in the Soviet way – I consult the people.'[35] (N.B. The Russian brings out the ontological argument of Grachikov here: 'Soviet' = 'Council'.) This is important for Solzhenitsyn because he shares the Actonian belief that all power tends to corrupt. When, for example, Vera Gangart appoints Kostoglotov 'senior patient', he enquires, 'are you trying to deal me an irreparable moral blow?'[36] Moreover, there are of course especial dangers for governments which are isolated from their people, and at the same time claim infallibility. In the prose poem 'Lake Segden', Solzhenitsyn underlines the total isolation of Stalin, so that he becomes a kind of inhuman ogre and at the same time is unable to adapt to changing circumstances. 'Man or beast, faced by that sign [No entry] must turn back. Some earthly power has put that sign there; past it none may ride, none may walk, crawl, or fly.'[37] (N.B. The Russian stresses the element of 'it is forbidden'.)

However, at the same time, this power referred to is also an 'earthly' power; and must therefore be fallible. This creates problems when members of the party and government commit mistakes, as Rusanov in *Cancer Ward* acknowledges in reference to Beria, his former 'boss'. (Rusanov's son Yuri carries the now malodorous name.)

All right, let's suppose Beria was a double dealer, a bourgeois nationalist and seeker after power. Very well, put him on trial and shoot him behind closed door, but why tell the ordinary people anything about it? Why shake their faith? Why create doubt in their minds?[38]

One may note in passing that it is precisely this problem which stands at the root of the process of re-Stalinisation today. As the official histories argue increasingly forcefully, Stalin himself must be seen as almost always *correct* in his actions. Once infallibility has been claimed, it becomes inseparable from the *legitimacy* of the government and the party. This is indeed dangerous, as Solzhenitsyn points out.

Solzhenitsyn gives convincing reasons for referring to the Soviet system of government as patrimonial. In the novella *For the Good of the Cause*, the decision to remove the new college buildings from the purlieu of the Institute is apparently a move to improve the *status* of the 'oblast', Knorozov's fiefdom, by attracting the prestigious new research centre into the region. It will be run for the greater glory of a local official (Khabalygin), and this turns out to be the real 'cause' for which

* The obkom is the Party Committee of the 'oblast' – a very important level in the Soviet hierarchy. The oblast is about the size of an American state.

the idealism and enthusiasm of the schoolchildren is being sacrificed. As Grachikov argues, 'We're not mediaeval barons trying to outdo each other by adding more quarterings to our coats of arms!'[39] Moreover, the sheer strength of the government to enforce its orders does not make them right; indeed, therein lies the dangerous principle of Thrasymachus in Plato's *Republic*, which incidentally can be easily refuted. (See Plato's *Republic*, Book 1.) And this, precisely, is the issue at stake. As Solzhenitsyn writes in his Open Letter to the All-Russian Patriarch, Pimen,

> In the end, the true and profound destiny of our country rests on this crucial point: will the idea be consolidated in public opinion that Might is Right? Or will it be purified of this darkness and will once again the Might of Justice begin to shine?[40]

Solzhenitsyn believes that all individuals have an ultimate value in themselves – a point which seems to me implicit in his very style of writing, so often 'polyphonic', that is, where each character steps to the front of the stage in turn as the action centres on him or her. Solzhenitsyn points with some finality to the fact of the loneliness of death. He rejects the idea that any materialist philosophy or any collective ethic can answer this final problem for the individual. Modern society may try to forget about death – as Solzhenitsyn records in his prose poem, '*We* will never die' – but as the sudden danger of mortal illness strikes such people as Dr Dontsova in *Cancer Ward*, this 'confirmed Oreshchenkov's opinion that modern man is helpless when confronted with death.'[41] Once again, Kostoglotov has the final word: 'what do we keep telling a man all his life? – "You're a member of the collective. You're a member of the collective!" He may be a member, but he has to die alone.' (N.B. The Russian accentuates the contrast between *membership* of the group and the solitary confrontation with death.)[42]

SUMMARY

Although Solzhenitsyn is primarily concerned with the destiny of his own country, and explanation of its post-revolutionary history, he is also a writer of universal human significance. He believes that man is a creature of unique significance and value in the natural world. Among the distinguishing features of man are his conscience and his ability to recognise what is just. Man is also possessed of free will and is not merely 'determined' by his social, economic or class background. Solzhenitsyn believes that each human personality has some kind of eternal value, or soul, and appears to support the view that each person has natural rights. People can only be truly free, and states can only be said to be free, when they respect these natural rights of human beings. Solzhenitsyn also rejects any censorship or controls on freedom of thought; likewise he opposes 'official' ideologies and indeed denies the possibility of formulating any totally satisfactory and permanent ideology.

The imposition of Marxism–Leninism in the USSR has created mediocre literature and stifled talent; moreover it is an inhuman and dangerous philosophy because it preaches, not the unit and harmony of mankind, but class warfare and class revenge in an age of nuclear weapons.

Solzhenitsyn does not welcome every aspect of modern life. He believes that a modern urban environment is noisy, dirty and distracting. He opposes trends in modern medicine which rely on drugs to suppress symptoms rather than attempting to create health. He is particularly opposed to the rapid industrialisation and socialism as experienced in the Soviet Union. Finally, he praises human character and achievement, including moral achievement, as the highest goal, and believes that government should be so organised that this becomes possible. For example, Solzhenitsyn advocates government as far as possible, by consent. He praises the small community and industry, respect for nature and the environment, and a more human tempo of life which might enable people to relate better to one another, being more aware of one another's personalities and mortality.

NOTES
1   *Sob. Soch.*, Vol. 6, p. 34.
2   *Sob. Soch.*, Vol. 5, pp. 269–70.
3   *Ibid.*, p. 84.
4   *Sob. Soch.*, Vol. 4, p. 696.
5   *Ibid.*, p. 716.
6   *Ibid.*, p. 561.
7   *Sob. Soch.*, Vol. 1, p. 28.
8   *Sob. Soch.*, Vol. 2, p. 534.
9   *Ibid.*, p. 475.
10   *Ibid.*, p. 89.
11   *Sob. Soch.*, Vol. 3, p. 236.
12   Solzhenitsyn became a member of Sakharov's Human Rights Committee in 1970.
13   *Sob. Soch.*, Vol. 4, p. 483.
14   Labedz, *Solzhenitsyn – A Documentary Record*, Penguin, (1974), p. 220.
15   Labedz, *ibid.*, pp. 106–12.
16   *Sob. Soch.*, Vol. 1, p. 245.
17   *Sob. Soch.*, Vol. 2, p. 139. The Russian text includes only the comment: 'Dyomke strashnovato stanovilos' chto pisatelei tak mnogo'. A paragraph is inserted in the English text (Penguin, 1968).
18   *Sob. Soch.*, Vol. 6, p. 249.
19   *Ibid.*, p. 51.
20   *Sob. Soch.*, Vol. 5, p. 221.

21   *Sob. Soch.*, Vol. 2. The Russian emphasises the pointlessness of such speed:
     'Vsegda vcem nikogda! Tselye zhizni nado reshat' v odnomu minutu.'
22   *Sob. Soch.*, Vol. 3, p. 333.
23   *Sob. Soch.*, Vol. 2, p. 92.
24   *Sob. Soch.*, Vol. 5, p. 225.
25   *Sob. Soch.*, Vol. 1, p. 199.
26   *Ibid.*, pp. 218–19.
27   *Sob. Soch.*, Vol. 2, p. 301.
28   *Sob. Soch.*, Vol. 4, pp. 411–12.
29   *Sob. Soch.*, Vol. 2, p. 166.
30   *Sob. Soch.*, Vol. 3, p. 293.
31   *Sob. Soch.*, Vol. 4, p. 544.
32   *Sob. Soch.*, Vol. 1, p. 231.
33   *Ibid.*, p. 113.
34   *Ibid.*, p. 267.
35   *Ibid.*
36   *Sob. Soch.*, Vol. 2, p. 248.
37   *Sob. Soch.*, Vol. 5, pp. 221–2. The Russian text is: 'ekhat' nel'zya i letet' nel'zya,
     idti nel'zya i polzti nel'zya'.
38   *Sob. Soch.*, Vol. 2, p. 207.
39   *Sob. Soch.*, Vol. 1, p. 283.
40   Lenten letter to the Patriarch Pimen, p. 2.
41   *Sob. Soch.*, Vol. 2, p. 496.
42   *Ibid.*, pp. 158–9. The Russian text is: 'Chlen-to on chlen, a umirat' emu odnomu'.

8 Internationalism, the nation in history, and the obligations of individuals

In this chapter I aim to identify (although I cannot entirely resolve) some apparent confusions in Solzhenitsyn's political thought. Firstly, there is the apparent difficulty of reconciling Solzhenitsyn's deep sense of patriotism with his evident concern for the 'common humanity' of man, and the high esteem in which he holds the term 'cosmopolitan'. Secondly, there is the problem of reconciling his views about the inscrutability of history with his evident desire to understand some of the historical processes which precede the rise of Soviet Russia and Stalinism. Thirdly, there is the difficulty of reconciling the belief that history proceeds according to its own 'organic' laws with the conviction that the individual can significantly change the course of history. Lastly, there is the problem of how the individual should act today in the face of a regime he regards as an historical catastrophe, and which is bent on his persecution.

Dealing first of all with Solzhenitsyn's deep love for his native land, it is evident that for him, Russia is both a source of inspiration and some kind of a healing, soothing environment, without which he cannot easily write and create. In *Matryona's Home*, we are told that the narrator 'just wanted to creep away and vanish in the very heartland of Russia – if there were such a place'.[1] Here there is an element of the legendary and the romantic which one associates with Slavophilism, or to be more accurate, the Native Soil Movement* (pochvennichestvo), as also in this passage, 'Tal'novo, Chaslitsy, Shestimirovo. . . . The names wafted over me like a soothing breeze. They held a promise of the true, legendary Russia.'[2] Solzhenitsyn's refusal to leave his country to collect his Nobel Prize in 1970, on the grounds that he might not be allowed to return, is well known. (And his subsequent expulsion from the Soviet Union in 1974 seems to prove that these fears were justified.) This refusal appears almost instinctive, as in the strangely relevant prose poem 'The bonfire and the ants', in which Solzhenitsyn relates the

* See Chapter 14.

episode of an old log being placed on a forest bonfire. The ants living in the log at first try to flee, but they 'no sooner overcame their terror than they turned and circled, and some kind of force drew them back to their forsaken homeland'.[3] (N.B. The Russian text specifically uses the word 'Rodina', 'Motherland'.) This concern for the homeland goes hand in hand with a deep love for the simple Russian people, who are portrayed as individuals rather than in some collective form as the 'narod'. For example, Zakhar Kalita is literally the guardian of part of the national heritage, the monument at Kulikovo field. Modern Russians, in a manner not unlike some modern English or Americans, had carved their names on this monument and generally vandalised it. Zakhar says, 'Have a look and see if you can read any of the dates. If you find any new damage, then you can blame me.'[4]

Alongside this patriotism, Solzhenitsyn is deeply concerned with the common humanity of man. In one sense, this quality of perceptive and compassionate humanism is pervasive in all Solzhenitsyn's writings, but he sometimes refers to the desirability of cosmopolitanism explicitly, as for example in *The First Circle* when he bemoans the campaign against the Jews ('rootless cosmopolitans') associated with Stalin's last years: 'this noble word ['cosmopolitan'], formerly used to denote the unity of the whole world, this proud title given only to the most universal geniuses . . . suddenly became mean, crabbed, and vicious. . . .'[5] Similarly, the communist patriot Rubin while studying Germany and conducting propaganda warfare against the German forces, comes to understand them, even in one sense 'becoming one of them'.[6]

It seems to me that the resolution of this apparent dilemma is possibly along these lines: patriotism, in the form of a profound love for one's native country, as opposed to any militarist jingoism, is for Solzhenitsyn an inspiration to creative literature and appreciation of beauty. As such it can be seen as a noble emotion, which raises up the spirit of man and inspires him, thereby enabling him in some way to enrich the human race as a whole.

However, at times this patriotism makes heavy demands on people. Whereas previously I have underlined Solzhenitsyn's demands for the establishment and preservation of individual *rights*, it is nevertheless the case that Solzhenitsyn also asks that people should acknowledge certain obligations. In time of war, Solzhenitsyn believes that a man must be ready to die for his country, since otherwise he cannot preserve his self-respect, or (more importantly) the nation will be defeated. Once again, a concern for the place of Russia in history is evident, combined with a belief which may be termed Gumploviczian (or Churchillian), that history is formed by nations victorious in war. As Varsonofiev says in *August 1914* in answer to Kotya's question, 'is it right to go to war?': 'I must say – yes, it is. . . . I can't prove it, but I feel it. When the trumpet sounds, a man must be a man, even if only for his self-respect. For some reason it is important that Russia's backbone shouldn't be broken.[7] Solzhenitsyn stresses the inherent toughness of Russians, which he brings out in his descriptions of men under fire in the East Prussian campaign, as compared with the inefficiency and cowardice of the High Command. He believes that this toughness is somehow derived from the national environment, as for example when Nerzhin reflects on the landscape study painted by Kondrashov-Ivanov in *The First Circle*. 'This Russia of ours is not as tame as it looks! It will not submit! It has never meekly accepted the Tartar yoke! It fights back!'[8]

On a less dramatic note, Solzhenitsyn demands that people should also recognise their social obligations to improve themselves, their *own* characters and minds. Only thus, he believes, can the human race, in its national communities, progress. Progress cannot be achieved by any sudden transformation of society, by for example such panaceas as changing the 'relations of production', or even (perhaps) equality of income distribution. This gradualist attitude towards social improvement is thus directly critical of the militant populism of Narodnaya Volya, and even, I think, of the Lavrovist philosophy of the intelligentsia's duty and moral, educative role in relation to the peasantry. Solzhenitsyn would, I believe, argue rather in the tone of the 'Vekhi' writers (liberals of 1909, including such people as Berdyayev, Gershenzon, Frank and Struve) that the intelligentsia should first look to themselves before seeking to improve others. As Varsonofiev puts it,

> Don't the people have any *obligations*? Or do they only have *rights*? Are they simply meant to sit and wait while we first supply them with happiness . . . ? And what if the people themselves aren't ready? Because if they aren't, then neither food, nor education, nor a change of institutions will be of any use.[9]

For Solzhenitsyn, then, the processes of history are complex and tortuous; and the progress of mankind possible, but inevitably very slow and long-term in producing improvements of any kind over a period of several generations. In trying to comprehend some of these processes, Solzhenitsyn encounters his next dilemma, neatly summarised here by Varsonofiev: 'History is *irrational*, young men. It has its own, and to us perhaps incomprehensible organic structure.' He said this, we are told, 'with despair'.[10] Solzhenitsyn's driving curiosity to understand the 'causes of things' is expressed in this passage from *Zakhar Kalita*: 'We wanted to understand the battle of Kulikovo in its entirety, grasp its inevitability, ignore the infuriating ambiguities of the chronicles: nothing had been as simple or as straightforward as it seemed.'[11] Solzhenitsyn is concerned that we should understand our past, and that it should all have some significance which serves to justify it. He is very concerned that the sacrifices of Russians, the wartime spirit and the friendship of soldiers should not vanish for ever and be forgotten, like smoke from an old trench bucket (*The Old Bucket*[12]). At the same time, Solzhenitsyn emphatically rejects Marxist conceptions of historical materialism and the 'inevitability' of social processes, but at the same time he seems to believe that history has a certain pattern. (Michael Glenny[13] has pointed out the fundamental incompatibility of Solzhenitsyn's views with those of Marxist–Leninists in this matter, and even more so with the claims of Soviet historiography.)

This 'pattern' of history is never entirely clear, but Solzhenitsyn seems on occasions to say that it may be intuited. As Varsonifiev puts it, 'when things are too clear they are no longer interesting. You see, the more important something is, the more impenetrable it seems.'[14] Impressionism may be used by the careful historian to portray the truth as art, or in riddles. Thus partial glimpses may be gained of a region otherwise inaccessible. By the term 'impressionism' I mean Solzhenitsyn's use of newspaper headlines and advertisements to convey the spirit of the times, and the use of 'film screen' techniques to convey an overall impression not easily conveyed by the printed word. Solzhenitsyn makes use of Russian folklore riddles to convey dimensions of meaning similarly inaccessible by other means. As is inscribed at the end of chapter 42 of *August 1914*, 'The answer to a riddle is short, but there are seven leagues of truth in it.'[15]

Dealing next with Solzhenitsyn's conception of the role of the individual in history, there is one sense in which the whole of *August 1914* can be seen as a dialogue (both actual, through the medium of Isaaki, and implicit throughout) with the ideas of Tolstoi. In this sense, Solzhenitsyn's relationship to Tolstoi may be compared with Max Weber's relationship to Marx. Like Weber, Solzhenitsyn asserts the importance of the individual and of ideas as opposed to the blind forces of history so evident, in their separate ways, in the philosophies of Tolstoi and Marx.

How, then, can the individual become effective in history? The fate of General Samsonov seems in one way to confirm Tolstoi's fatalism, an attitude which Samsonov himself adopts when paying his last respects to his defeated army. He is the largely innocent recipient of a dangerous strategic situation coupled with the outmoded military methods and supply systems of the Russian Army. He is moreover surrounded by an inefficient and inexperienced staff, and directed by the malicious and incompetent Zhilinskii in matters where his command overlaps with that of the General Staff. However, it soon becomes clear that what he lacks is adequate information, both as regards his own troops and in terms of reconnaissance of the Germans. He also lacks a clear picture of the strategic position as a whole. Samsonov lacks information, but he also lacks the intuition of General von François or of his own subordinate General Martos. Such people can, apparently, change the situation fundamentally, but they have to be in the correct location in the hierarchy of command, and possessed of a certain independence of mind as well as a lot of information and experience. Leadership is also important, and can be effective in altering strategic and crucial historical occurrences, as for example when 'the bright flame of Vorotyntsev's self-confidence kindled the senior officers of the Rifle Brigade into life'.[16] The importance of being in the right place at the right time seems to impress Solzhenitsyn: High Commands and General Staffs are usually, it seems, too remote or too preoccupied with political rivalries to be properly placed – Ludendorff and Hindenburg do not show up particularly well even when compared with the 'Stavka' of the Grand Duke Nicholas. However, such men as Martos, when in command of a situation they understand and operating with staff and troops who are known and trusted, can be very successful. But when Martos is transferred, he loses his effectiveness.

The other generals under Samsonov's command represent various attitudes towards the role of individual action and initiative. Obviously the slight misinterpretation of Kutuzov's views (as portrayed by Tolstoi) embraced by General Blagoveshchenskii is disastrous. 'His long military service had convinced the General of the correctness of Tolstoi's views; there is nothing worse than sticking one's neck out and using one's initiative – people who did so always got into trouble.'[17] Similarly, the 'petty tutelage' of the ubiquitous Artamanov is quite ineffective and even dangerous, as is the pettyfogging bureaucracy of Postovskii. The dangers of being carried along by events, by the 'organic' laws of history, are indeed great, and Samsonov's final prayer for forgiveness illustrates the inevitability of his fate: 'O Lord, if Thou can'st, forgive me and receive me. Thou seest – I could do no other, and can do no other now.'[18] We are told that 'he groaned aloud like any dying creature of the forest.'[19] He is dying like an animal, and he has lost that precious gift of free will and free action which only human beings, as opposed to animals, possess, albeit in small measure.

The difficulty of interpreting history resides not only in the problem of locating the role of individual action, but because history operates like a living, organic process which functions according to its own laws; 'if you prefer,' says Varsonofiev,

history is a river; it has its own laws which govern its flow, its bends, the way it meanders. . . . And we're told that the bed must be forcibly diverted by several thousand yards. The bonds between generations, bonds of institution, tradition, custom – are what hold the banks of the river bed together and keep the stream flowing.[20]

This view of history is (surely) remarkably similar to that of Edmund Burke, who rejects the notion of 'social contract' as outlined by such writers as Jean-Jacques Rousseau, arguing that the bonds of custom and tradition tend to weld national life in some organic way which links one's ancestors with the living and those as yet unborn. Similarly, for Solzhenitsyn, the 'social order' is not susceptible of exact analysis, although he does concede that

> obviously one kind [of society] is less evil than all others. Perhaps there may even be a perfect one. Only remember, my friends, that the best social order is not susceptible of being arbitrarily constructed, nor even of being scientifically constructed.[21]

Solzhenitsyn's attitudes as regards political institutions are also quite Burkean, or perhaps within the Russian context comparable with the ideas of D. N. Shipov. Like Burke and Shipov, Solzhenitsyn sees institutions as the product of evolution over a long period of national history: for otherwise they lack any substance or life of their own in the national consciousness. Like Varsonofiev, Solzhenitsyn rejects notions of the 'People's Power'[22] (N.B. Michael Glenny oddly translates this as 'democracy') and also the notion of a blueprint constitution, which devises new institutions to express such concepts as People's Power.

> Who is conceited enough to imagine that he can actually devise ideal institutions? The only people who think they can are those who believe that nothing significant was ever done before their own time, that their generation will be the first to achieve anything worthwhile.[23]

Solzhenitsyn, like Shipov, believes that religion has a profoundly humanising effect on men's actions and their beliefs. In the prose poem 'Journey down the Oka', Solzhenitsyn remarks that the soothing effect of the Central Russian countryside is largely due to the churches.

> People have always been selfish and often evil. But the angelus used to toll and its echo would float over village, field and wood. It reminded man that he must abandon his trivial earthly cares and give up one hour of his thoughts to life eternal. The tolling of the eventide bell (which now survives for us only in popular song) raised man above the level of a beast.[24]

Hence, as in the philosophy of Burke, any attempt to make a sudden change in the social structure, as for example in revolution, is not only dangerous but also destructive – perhaps in some way obstructive of divine law?

Varsonofiev has some comments to make about sharp breaks with the past: 'the State does not like a sharp break with the past. It favours gradualism. A sudden change, a leap forward, is destructive of the State.'[25] (N.B. Michael Glenny's translation is a little free here: 'skachok' means 'break' or 'leap', not necessarily 'leap forward'.)

Finally, it is necessary to resolve the dilemma of the evolutionary conservative in a post-revolutionary situation, if this be possible. The difference between Solzhenitsyn and Edmund Burke lies essentially in their tone of voice. Burke can still employ an easy 'establishment' tone, comparing for example the demands of the French Revolutionary 'Cabals' to the insignificant croakings of grasshoppers in an English meadow.[26] Solzhenitsyn's persecuted voice is that of minority opposition, and it is this, together with his specifically Russian and Slavophile orientation, which brings to mind D. N. Shipov, sometime leader of the Octobrist Party in the Imperial Russian Duma. Shipov's rather non-Slavophile emphasis on regular political activity and his political programme (the 'Twenty Points'[27]) have not as yet been directly matched by Solzhenitsyn (unless one can cite the 'Letter to Soviet Leaders'), who has always stressed the subordinate nature of politics for him as compared with his art. However, as Peter Reddaway points out,[28] Solzhenitsyn's honorary membership of Academician Sakharov's human rights committee is a very significant step in the direction of 'legal' political action, as also is the publication of *Gulag Archipelago* and subsequent articles and protests since his explusion from the Soviet Union. Solzhenitsyn hoped at one time that the present regime would change its structure from within over a period of time, as shown in his 'Letter to Soviet Leaders'. But as the Soviet leaders pursue even more vigorously the process of historical reaction which is termed re-Stalinisation, this final question of Solzhenitsyn becomes at the same time more urgent and terrifying. 'And what of our disastrous, chaotic lives? What of our explosions of protest, the groans of men shot by firing squads, the tears of our women; will all this too – terrible thought – be utterly forgotten?' ('The City on the Neva').[29]

SUMMARY

In Soviet Marxism, the words 'patriot', 'nationalist', '(great-power) chauvinist', have become inextricably confused. Even in contemporary Western thought, especially in liberal-left circles, the concepts have become somewhat synonymous, and anyone who claims to be patriotic is often misinterpreted. Solzhenitsyn's nationalism is not by any means a form of Great Russian nationalism or chauvinism, but he does have a profound love of Russia (as opposed to the Soviet Union), and he suggests that love of one's home country, history and culture is a very widespread and powerful emotion among people of all nations. As far as Solzhenitsyn is concerned, that is a noble emotion which need not discount cosmopolitan ideals or an internationalist orientation, which he esteems very highly. He believes that individuals have a duty to develop themselves (their talents and characters) and that they have to be prepared to die for their country in wartime. This is an apparent problem of Solzhenitsyn's thought because presumably his reasoning would apply in exactly the same way to Germany in the First World War, for example.

Solzhenitsyn believes that the role of the individual in history is obscure but meaningful if the person concerned acts according to his conscience and to the best of his abilities, which should be developed to their highest extent. *August 1914* may be seen in one sense as an essay on the mysterious theme of the individual's role in history. He believes that history is not entirely inscrutable, and that its processes may be intuitively grasped or partially apprehended by the careful and thorough researcher.

Solzhenitsyn rejects ideas of any 'social contract' and views national history as a unique evolution based on custom and tradition. He has some affinities here with Burke and English Conservative thought. In the Russian context, it might be possible to draw parallels between Solzhenitsyn and the ideas of D. N. Shipov, who was the first leader of the Octobrist Party in the Imperial Duma. Like Burke and Shipov, Solzhenitsyn believes that Christianity is the only possible basis for civilised and humane society. Finally, Solzhenitsyn is by nature an evolutionist, and opposes all forms of revolution; but he sees no hope of compromise with the Soviet leaders.

NOTES

1   *Sob. Soch.*, Vol. 1, p. 195.
2   *Ibid.*, p. 197.
3   *Sob. Soch.*, Vol. 5, p. 226.
4   *Sob. Soch.*, Vol. 1, p. 299. Later (p. 303), Zakhar is referred to as a 'kind of guardian angel, who never left the place'.
5   *Sob. Soch.*, Vol. 4, p. 588.
6   *Sob. Soch.*, Vol. 3, p. 17.
7   *Avgust chetyrnadtsatovo*, Flegon Press (1971), p. 378.
8   *Sob. Soch.*, Vol. 3, p. 358.
9   *Avgust chetyrnadtsatovo*, *op. cit.*, p. 373.
10   *Ibid.*, p. 376.
11   *Sob. Soch.*, Vol. 1, p. 303.
12   A. Solzhenitsyn, *Stories and Prose Poems*, (trans. Michael Glenny), Bodley Head (1971), p. 235.
13   *Survey*, No. 83 (Spring 1972). Glenny writes: 'In setting out to refute the knowingly false Communist Party version of history and to reject the discredited historicism on which the present Soviet regime relies for its justification, Solzhenitsyn is aiming a blow not only at one of the ideological roots of the existing system but

more generally at the organised perversion of consciousness which has been the result of treating mankind as a mere object, as no more than fuel for driving the locomotive of history towards Communism' (p. 122).

14 *Avgust chetyrnadtsatovo, op. cit.*, pp. 370–1.
15 *Ibid.*, p. 379.
16 *August 1914*, Bodley Head (1972), p. 278.
17 *Ibid.*, p. 464.
18 *Avgust chetyrnadtsatovo, op. cit.*, p. 430.
19 *Ibid.*, p. 430.
20 *Ibid.*, p. 377.
21 *Ibid.*, p. 376.
22 *Ibid.*, p. 375. The Russian text is 'Chto zh po vashemu, narodovlastie – ne vysshaya forma pravleniya?'
23 *Ibid.*, p. 375.
24 *Sob Soch.*, Vol. 5, p. 232.
25 *Avgust chetyrnadtsatovo, op. cit.*, p. 370. The Russian text is 'A gosudarstvo – ono ne lyubit rezkogo razryva s proshlym. Ono imenno postepennost' lyubit. Pereryv, skachok, eto dlya nevo rasrushitel'no.'
26 E. Burke, *Reflections on the Revolution in France*, Pelican (1968), p. 82.
27 L. B. Schapiro, *Rationalism and Nationalism in Nineteenth-Century Russian Political Thought*, Yale University Press (1967), final chapter. See also D. N. Shipov, *Memoirs*, Moscow (1918).
28 P. Reddaway (ed.), *Uncensored Russia*, Jonathan Cape (1972).
29 *Sob. Soch.*, Vol. 5, p. 226.

9 Literary postscript

Solzhenitsyn's uncompromising opposition to the present Soviet regime has become much clearer since his enforced exile in the West, not only through public statements and television appearances such as the 'Panorama' interview on BBC-1 (1 March 1976) but also because his total published works are now coming to light. For example, we now know the extent to which the Soviet-published texts of *One Day in the Life of Ivan Denisovich* and *Matryona's Home* were censored in the USSR, and certain general conclusions about the reasons for this censorship are possible. Moreover, the missing chapters of *The First Circle* are gradually appearing in the West, and these indicate some of Solzhenitsyn's more uncompromising views. Finally, in March 1976 the third 'book' (Parts V–VII) of *Gulag Archipelago* appeared relating the nightmares of the Soviet camp experience to the fifties and the sixties, a period which includes the rule of the present leadership (Brezhnev).

Firstly, Soviet censorship of Solzhenitsyn's works published in the USSR indicate that the authorities must have been wary of Solzhenitsyn's philosophy from the early sixties, and the censored passages themselves show us something of the motivations and outlook of officialdom, and what that officialdom was concerned to hide. A valuable piece of research by T. Weiss of Radio Liberty[1] has revealed much in this area. Apparently, in the published Soviet version of *One Day in the Life of Ivan Denisovich* there were no fewer than 34 omitted passages, 33 substitutions and six additions. The omissions were mainly references by Shukhov to his former life on the kolkhoz (collective farm). For example, when Shukhov has to choose between felt boots (valenki) and leather boots, he reluctantly gave up his leather ones. All the boots were thrown in a heap 'in the same way as they drove horses into the kolkhoz' (i.e. in the collectivisation drive in the thirties). This passage is deleted. Shukhov goes on to say that 'he also had a gelding before the kolkhozes. He took good care of him, but then the strangers ruined him in no time.' This, too, is deleted. So is the passage in a letter from his wife which says that women who failed to fulfil their work norms on the kolkhoz were to be put in prison, but that this threat was not carried out. There is in addition a passage in which Shukhov muses to himself, 'The kolkhoz has been kept alive by the same women who were there since the thirties, and when they fall dead the kolkhoz will also kick the bucket.' Here the secondary clause is deleted, and a change inserted so that the post-censorship sentence reads, 'The kolkhoz has been kept alive by the same women who were driven into the kolkhoz since the 1930s.' Shukhov's wife apparently advised him in the original version not to return to the kolkhoz, and says that a lot of the men made their money by printing and selling carpets. The advice not to return is deleted, as are some of Shukhov's thoughts about the possibility of earning his living this way if he is deprived of rights of residence after his release. Shukhov thinks to himself as follows (censored passages are in brackets): 'a return to a straight life was blocked [by the authorities] but people still didn't get lost; they found ways to get around [restrictions] and make a living that way.' Shukhov refers here to such alternatives as truck driving, heavy equipment operating, free-work in camps.

Team-leader Tyurin's memories about 'the annihilation of the kulaks as a class' are greatly cut. He reports that after his expulsion from the army because of his kulak origins, he made it down to the railway station, where he saw a terrible sight. This 'sight' is deleted: 'The whole square around the station was thickly covered by the greatcoats of peasants. Their owners had starved to death, since they could not get away.' A scene depicting the fear of hunted kulak children is also deleted.[2] There are many other deletions, including any acrimonious remarks about Soviet bureaucracy, treatment of Soviet 'returnees' from Germany and annexations of parts of Poland (changed to 'Western Ukraine'). Weiss summarises: 'in general, the censors eliminated anything that might indicate any defiance or feeling of revenge on the part of prisoners, or of the people.'[3]

Dealing with *substitutions* in the texts, these are sometimes just fillings, in order to make sense of the deleted sentences, but more often they have a positive intent, being designed to smooth over any abrasive comments or rough episodes. For example, back in the kolkhoz, Shukhov remembers that one had to 'grease palms' in order to get through, including on occasions to 'give a bribe to the police'. Here, the word 'police' is omitted and 'someone' is substituted. When Shukhov refers to the bread ration, Shukhov says: 'two times a day, when they got their bread rations'. The censored version reads: '*every time,* when they got their bread rations'. Also, the colourful 'zek' terminology is toned down throughout: For example, the word *podukhat'* ('to kick the bucket') is replaced by the standard *pogibat'* ('to perish').

The *additions* seem to be purposeful: for example, when Buinovskii shouts that stripping men in the cold is against the rules, 'You are not Soviet people,' the censor adds another sentence, 'You are not communists.' The meaning here is perhaps to suggest Buinovskii's error –

real communists would not treat people this way. This seems to be in line with Khrushchev's general policy on the subject of Stalin and his camps, namely that despite Stalin, the *Communist Party* remained on the right course.

The principles applied to the censoring of *Matryona's Home* were similar, in trying to limit the story to immediate issues only, cutting down its general meaning and generally blunting its impact. The very first sentence is changed: 'On the one hundred and eighty-fourth kilometre from Moscow, on the connecting line to Murom and Kazan' – the section after the comma is omitted. Also the timing is changed: Solzhenitsyn's story is set in 1956, but the censor dates it before 1953. The suggestion is that the camps (from where the narrator is coming) were closed immediately after Stalin's death.

The fact that Matryona's garden was cut down to a small plot, and she was still obliged to work on the kolkhoz for this, is deleted. Also her opinions about the lack of incentives to work on the kolkhoz are censored. There is censorship and deletion in the matter of Matryona's pension rights: apparently the new pension law (under Khrushchev) was aimed at limiting pensions to the former members of the kolkhoz. This excluded Matryona: ' "And what is that new pension?" others objected. "The state can change its mind any minute. Today they give it to you, and take it away tomorrow." '[4] Any passages indicating religious *habits* are deleted. The sentence 'She always had consecrated water at home, but for this year she remained without any' was cut out.[5] Similarly the sentence about Matryona's ikons is changed. Matryona had 'a sacred corner in the good room of the house, and another one at the ikon of Nikolai-the-miracle-worker in the kitchen.' The censor summed up the information as 'There were ikons in the house.'[6] Finally Matryona's disparaging comments about the content of Soviet radio programmes and about artificial satellites are deleted.

Soviet authorities were careful about publishing the talented works of Solzhenitsyn, and he too attempted not so much to tone down his writing as to publish only what he thought the censorship might conceivably accept. For this purpose, he deliberately excluded certain chapters from the novels *The First Circle* and *August 1914*. I deal with the exclusion from *August 1914* in chapter 12. The missing chapters from *The First Circle* are now (1975–6) gradually appearing. I deal here with four chapters only out of the nine: chapters 44 ('Out in the open'), 61 ('The uncle from Tver'), 88 ('Dialectical materialism') and 90 ('The word will break the concrete'). These chapters have appeared in consecutive numbers of *The Herald of the Russian Christian Movement*, starting with No. 111 (1974), and in *Kontinent*, starting with No. 1 (1974). The series is not yet complete (March 1976).

Chapter 44 of *The First Circle* describes a scene which takes place between Innokenti Volodin and Klara Makarygin. The action takes place in 1949, five years after Klara had noticed the 'charlady' working on the staircase of the privileged Makarygin apartment and had come to realise that the Soviet system depended upon the labour of prisoners. She seeks to find out more about this, and about life in the West, from Innokenti the Soviet diplomat. Innokenti, who is her brother-in-law, unexpectedly confesses his love for Klara, and they decide to take a train 'anywhere' from the Kiev station in Moscow. The train turns out to be bound for a place called 'Nara', which is a bad omen, because Klara's sister, Innokenti's wife, is called Nara for short. En route, Innokenti analyses a copy of *Pravda* for Klara, exposing the lies, distortions and half-truths. On being asked, what can be done, he replies 'I don't know.' They alight from the train on a whim, and follow an old peasant woman out of the station. They are surprised to discover a lyrical scene, a meadow and an old cemetery. They resolve to walk to the forest, but come first to a dilapidated village. Here Solzhenitsyn compares the beauty of the countryside with the squalor of Russian rural life: the village, Rozhdestvo ('Christmas') is filthy, its road a mass of potholes and mud, despoiled by caterpillar tracks and heavy vehicles, while its church is now a kolkhoz depot. A peasant cadges cigarettes, while Innokenti muses on the corrupt affluence of the Western Christmas and the desecrated church of the Eastern Christmas.

Klara and Innokenti try to get to the forest by following a stream, but come across another broken-down kolkhoz depot, and then a metalled highway with a convoy of over a hundred military vehicles. This is a crucial part of the couple's picture of Russian reality. Innokenti feels that there are two important circles of existence: first, one's fatherland; second, humanity. However, in Russia there is no proper communication between the two, because 'there is a fence of prejudices. There are barbed wires with machine guns. Neither the heart nor the soul can get through here.'[7] They discover in Russia only ugliness, and fail on a personal level to find any way out for their relationship. Loneliness and ultimate disaster is to be their lot.

This chapter is an important one, especially in the development of Volodin, for the Christmas phone call, in which he tried to warn his friend about impending arrest, is prefigured here. Also it brings out some of Solzhenitsyn's themes, many of which did not emerge until the publication of the 'Letter to Soviet Leaders' (1974): for example, destruction of the countryside under communist rule, excessive military expenditure, the lies of the press, destruction of churches, degradation of peasant life, distortion of relationships under the social system of the USSR, and the impossibility of detente.

Chapter 88[8] takes us to the Monday night just before the transfer of Nerzhin and other rebellious 'zeks' from Mavrino, the special camp for technically 'useful' prisoners which is described by Solzhenitsyn as *The First Circle*. There is a sarcastic comment that throughout the Soviet Union on Monday nights, people had to listen to political indoctrination – usually from the 'Short Course' History of the Party. On this particular night the chapter is definitely one of Stalin's own, the one on dialectical and historical materialism.[9] The lecturer is a certain Rakhmankul Shamsetdinov (obviously non-Russian), and Solzhenitsyn describes how he whipped through the material, which he evidently knew by heart, but at the same time made many mistakes, while all the distinguished scientists at Mavrino had to sit and listen to him. In reality, though, as Solzhenitsyn shows brilliantly well, neither they nor the lecturer nor the staff are really paying any attention at all. (The staff included Klara and Simochka, who are dreaming of their boyfriends Russka and Nerzhin.) This is a comment on the intellectual bankruptcy of Soviet Marxism, for Solzhenitsyn has depicted the session as a nonsensical ritual, a barren punishment for listeners and lecturer alike, having no relation to anyone's life. He contrasts the ideas of dialectical materialism with his underlying religious theme, showing materialism to be fundamentally anti-religious but failing to replace the moral content of religion with anything worthy of the name. (Compare Rubin's ludicrous experiments with 'civic temples' in chapter 67. The communist Rubin, having spent many years of life attacking church ritual, now proposed to prop up civic morality with some kind of solemn state ritual.)

In chapter 61[10] Innokenti, spurred on by Klara, travels to Tver to meet his only remaining relative on his mother's side, a mysterious uncle called 'Avenir', who lives in an apparently broken-down hut with old Soviet papers strewn about the place. This apparent disorganisation turns out to be a cleverly disguised archive. For example, if he was asked by an official, 'And why do you keep precisely this issue, citizen?', Uncle Avenir would answer, 'But I don't keep it, I just take them as they come.' Meanwhile, although it would have been dangerous to take notes, 'uncle remembered by heart where to look for what'.[11] The chapter takes the form of a monologue, and in some ways, once again, it resembles the content of the 'Letter to Soviet Leaders'. I think that the uncle may be seen as a portrait of Solzhenitsyn himself, working in secret at his historical studies. For example, the uncle puts forward the idea that the peasant's life is preferable to that of the urban worker; that the working class is not necessarily progressive; that industrialisation is not of great benefit; that women could easily change roles and go out to work while the man stays at home. (This last point sheds light on Solzhenitsyn's *real* attitude towards women's rights. See chapter 11.) Uncle Avenir suggests that modern urban dwelling and factory life are destructive of human relations and morality. He believes that people can no longer respect the Soviet government and that they obey only from fear. He shows Innokenti pictures of Stalin toasting Hitler (*Pravda* of 1940), and earlier editions in which Stalin is seen defending Kamenev and Zinoviev, whom he later killed. The basic tactic of the regime over many years, says Solzhenitsyn, has been deception, and now the people are aware of this to some extent. Avenir points out that at no time in the Tsarist period were repressions so onerous as those of the Soviet period. He stresses that the regime has always taken the most careful measures to protect itself, even in wartime, with widespread deployment of NKVD troops in every province. He argues that the Bolsheviks came to power illegally, as for example when there were only 330 out of 900 delegates present when the Soviet of People's Commissars was set up, and when the Constituent Assembly of January 1918 was forcibly disbanded by Bolshevik sharpshooters. (This was 'the first and only day of a free Russian parliament for the last five hundred years in history, and for another hundred ahead'.[12]) In an interesting aside, Avenir says, if the regime has the atomic bomb, 'we are done for, Innokenti. We'll never see freedom again.'[13] The implications of this remark seem to be that nuclear weapons must lead to stalemate at the very least in the strategic relation between East and West. Uncle Avenir also tells Innokenti about his parentage, facts not previously known to him: his father was apparently one of the Red Guards who had been involved in the subversion of the Constituent Assembly, while his mother had been sceptical about Bolshevik rule. Avenir thus points up the (biological) conflict which faces Innokenti, and the final words have an air of foreboding: 'Have you ever felt the truth of the saying that the sins of the parents will be visited on the children? . . . It is this that you have to cleanse yourself of.'[14]

Chapter 90[15] deals with another favourite theme of Solzhenitsyn: what is a *just* society, and how can the Soviet Union be transformed into one? The scene is an urgent discussion between Gerasimovich and Nerzhin. The former believes that it is possible to perfect society and that it should be run by a technical intelligentsia, an elite. Gerasimovich is opposed to democracy. Nerzhin, however, emphasises the need for ethical principles on the part of the people as well as the intelligentsia. He agrees that democracy in the Soviet Union is unworkable, and that political authority would be required, but not based solely on coercion: it should be a respected authority. He goes on to say,

But how do you get such a form of government? . . . since it easily can be said that authoritarianism soon turns into totalitarianism. If you ask me, I would rather have something like what Switzerland has. . . . The stronger the political power, the lower visibility it should have: the biggest unit should be the village commune . . . [but] after all isn't it too early for us to discuss such things? . . . Wouldn't it make more sense for us to discuss how we're going to get rid of an unreasonable form of organisation?[16]

If one may ascribe such views to Solzhenitsyn today, this is a fascinating comment on his politics, suggesting that he has some ideas about the necessary means for bringing the present regime to an end, but that his views about the desirable shape of the post-Soviet regime is as yet somewhat hazy. Gerasimovich has traditional ideas about how to achieve a *coup d'état*. He proposes the formation of a kind of Leninist-style group of a few thousand courageous men. He suggests that after such a coup, it might be necessary to kill some 5,000 people, including Molotov and Beria. But Nerzhin is pessimistic and opposed to such schemes. He feels that it would be difficult to find the required number of courageous men and to organise them. He is sceptical about physical revolution and violence, and he feels that outside help would not be forthcoming from the appeasement-minded West or from the USA. The West, he believes, is weakened by too much good living, has made too many concessions; and the Soviet people are too apathetic and demoralised, ruined by widespread alcoholism. Finally he envisages a nuclear war. 'Perhaps in a new era, a method will be discovered: the word will destroy the concrete. . . . Remember, "In the beginning was the Word. . . ." Which means that the Word is stronger than concrete.'[17]

This apocalyptic and mysterious prediction appears in a book which also predicted that the USA would be the first to achieve a manned flight to the moon: there is a prophetic element in Solzhenitsyn's writing. He goes on to say that whereas a few decades ago, the fearful atrocities of the middle years of the twentieth century would not have been thought possible, now we need to contemplate the possibility of nuclear war and the possibility of some kind of human life surviving in a more humane kind of society, where the ideas and actions of good men will become more influential. This passage gives us a clear indication of Solzhenitsyn's pessimism and the messianic traces which undoubtedly exist in his thoughts.

SUMMARY

Soviet censorship of Solzhenitsyn's works, and his own self-censorship, reveal much about Solzhenitsyn's relation to the regime and his real views. Soviet censors were afraid that some of Solzhenitsyn's views might be damaging to Soviet public opinion, and their extensive modification of Solzhenitsyn's texts, which must have been heart-breaking to the author, are an astonishing comment on contemporary Soviet practice as well as revealing that there must have been considerable opposition to the limited publication of Solzhenitsyn's work. In particular, the authorities were keen to cut out references to the disastrous consequences of collectivisation (including the neglect of livestock and reliance on women workers), and the cruelties of the collectivisation campaign and dekulakisation. In a narrowly bureaucratic way, disparaging references to the authorities were also removed, as were critical comments about the annexation of parts of Poland and the treatment of returnees from German camps. Additions were made to texts in order to suggest the correct political line of Khrushchev's time, namely that Stalin had been the root of all evil and that all abuses had ceased with his death under the guidance of the party, which was now fulfilling its programme including the industrial and technological transformation of the USSR and the elimination of religious prejudices.

Solzhenitsyn's 'missing' chapters indicate that for many years he has criticised Russian society along the lines expressed in the 'Letter to Soviet Leaders'. He points to the intellectual and moral bankruptcy of Soviet Marxism and the process of distortion of history which has become a distinguishing mark of the regime. He suggests that the nuclear age must mean that there is no hope of liberation of the USSR from without, but that nuclear war is still possible. Finally, like Nerzhin in *The First Circle*, Solzhenitsyn rejects all forms of physical or political opposition to the regime, and regards all definite political programmes of action as premature compared with the immediate task of moral regeneration and removal of the existing regime.

NOTES

1 *Radio Liberty Research Bulletin* (7 March 1975), T. Weiss (RL96/75).
2 *Ibid.*, p. 3.
3 *Ibid.*
4 *Ibid.*, p. 5.
5 *Ibid.*, p. 6.
6 *Ibid.*
7 *Vestnik Russkovo Khristianskovo Dvizheniya*, No. 111, p. 88.
8 *Kontinent*, No. 1 (1974).
9 *Istoriya KPSS: (b) Kratkii kurs* (1938), chapter 4.
10 *Vestnik . . .*, No. 112/13.
11 *Ibid.*, p. 167.
12 *Ibid.*, p. 171.
13 *Ibid.*, p. 169.
14 *Ibid.*, p. 173.
15 *Vestnik . . .*, No. 114, IV, pp. 193–203.
16 *Ibid.*, p. 197.
17 *Ibid.*, p. 203.

Part Two

MORAL AND POLITICAL ANALYSIS

10 The Nobel Prize speech: Repentance and self-limitation

In the autumn of 1970, Aleksandr Solzhenitsyn was awarded the Nobel Prize for (among other considerations) his part in continuing the 'indispensable traditions' of Russian literature and the 'moral force' of his writing. The authorities refused Solzhenitsyn permission to receive the prize on Russian soil, and the Swedish Embassy in Moscow apparently considered that any presentation at the embassy would be detrimental to relations with the Soviet Union. After some consideration, Solzhenitsyn had decided not to travel to Stockholm, because he feared, rightly it seems in the light of subsequent events, that he would not be allowed to return to his native land. His Nobel Prize speech was read in his absence.

This speech is perhaps the first explicit outline of Solzhenitsyn's philosophy of art, and relates this more clearly to his general world outlook. References to Dostoevskii are numerous in this document, and it seems that Solzhenitsyn's debate with the ghost of Tolstoi is now overshadowed by a new involvement with the profound moral and aesthetic philosophy of Dostoevskii. It is necessary to stress once again that Solzhenitsyn's starting point is not political ideas, but aesthetics and morality. He begins with Dostoevskii's 'mysterious' comment that 'the world will be saved by beauty'.

Art, says Solzhenitsyn, is as old as man; it is like a fairy-tale looking-glass, which reflects in some way aspects of the life of man but at the same time illumines them and gives them significance, some absolute meaning. What is more, he says, no *genuine* art allows 'strained invented concepts', for these 'do not withstand the image test'.[1] There is therefore more of truth to be found in art than in, for example, political manifestos, which may sound plausible and attractive but always tend towards bias in the name of success in the political struggle. It is not quite clear by what mechanisms art is inherently more truthful than a political philosophy or manifesto: I suspect that Solzhenitsyn would have sympathy with the Keatsian view that beauty and truth are synonymous. Art, says Solzhenitsyn, 'carries in itself its own checking system'.[2] However, as will become clearer in the next chapter, it must surely be acknowledged that Solzhenitsyn himself has a political programme. Its main outlines are contained in the 'Letter to Soviet Leaders'. Would Solzhenitsyn be prepared to regard these views as inherently biased and relative? It is true that many Western scholars, in particular Professor S. E. Finer, have stressed the element of 'pseudo-reasoning' to be found in conflicts between political opponents and in justification for a particular 'political formula'.[3] Nevertheless, the relation between truth and political thought is not adequately dealt with, so it seems, in Solzhenitsyn's published works to date (1975).

Solzhenitsyn nevertheless pursues his relentless quest for absolute standards of truth and justice. To follow his path is to become aware of his towering moral stature. He compares our appreciation of justice to the beating of one's heart; this analogy has already been mentioned above, and occurs in the 'Advice to Three Students'. Solzhenitsyn points out that different nations do not in fact *practise* justice as though it were an absolute standard. This, says Solzhenitsyn is perhaps understandable when national experience was widely divergent between nations which in former times had little mutual interaction and commerce. 'But now the whole human race is squeezed together into a single lump . . .',[4] and such differences about what constitutes justice and injustice can be (in some sense) fatal. The world is now united, he says, a single community; and comparing this community to a person, he points out that a man with two hearts is doomed.[5]

What then is the role of individual nations, and how can the art of one nation beneficially influence the human race? Solzhenitsyn has a subtle and original view of nations, which has been widely misunderstood.[6] He argues that nations have separate characters; each one is an individual, providing richness and variety in much the same way as individual people impart different colours, contributions, to human society. 'Nations are part of the wealth of the human race. Although generalised, they are its individuals. The smallest of them has its own special colours and hides in itself some special facet of God's design.'[7] Solzhenitsyn, then, would oppose those trends in modern society which might tend to *destroy* national cultures, such as the unchecked processes of international economic growth, and perhaps what Marcuse has called 'the totalitarian universe of technological rationality'.[8] He thinks that we should concentrate on the preservation and natural evolution of nations. This does not entitle his critics to call him 'chauvinist' or even 'nationalist', if that term is used in any pejorative sense. He is merely trying to come to terms with the continuing fact of the existence of strong national feelings in the twentieth century, but this does not preclude a nation's having an international outlook, foreign travel for its citizens and cultural interaction. Indeed the whole tenor of this Nobel Prize Speech is that the world community must now be seen as a whole. Finally Solzhenitsyn has great respect for the lofty ideals of cosmopolitanism and internationalism. In his article 'The smatterers' (which is dealt with more fully in the next chapter), he says: 'there is great spiritual nobility and beauty in it [the idea of internationalism] and mankind is probably destined one day to rise to those noble heights.'[9]

Since Solzhenitsyn wishes to preserve the national or cultural roots of each nation, he underlines the importance of national art for this purpose. 'Art preserves [the nation's] lost history in a form which is not subject to distortion and slander.'[10] But the national artist also has an international role. The establishment of basic, common standards of justice and human rights is not just a matter of international negotiation for the enforcement of (say) Article 19 of the UN Declaration on Human Rights. In the search for agreed standards, the artist and the writer have a unique role to play. In the first place they should expose the political slogans of 'class conflict, race war, the struggle of the masses, or the trade unions' as so much rationalisation of what in fact are 'the same old cave-man impulses – greed, envy, lack of restraint, mutual ill will . . .'.[11] In the second place artists and writers have an inescapable *duty* to speak out clearly. 'The writer . . . is not some casual judge of his fellow countrymen and his contemporaries. He is an accomplice in all the evil that is committed in his own country and by his own people.'[12] And in a clear reference to Czechoslovakia and Hungary he goes on to say, 'If the tanks of his country's army have bloodied the asphalt streets of another country's capital city, then those brown stains are spattered for ever over the face of the writer.'[13] This, surely, is the true voice of Russia's indispensable moral literary tradition.

In the third place national literature which is read internationally can educate people and illustrate vividly, in a way that no other medium can provide, the pains and sorrows, the agony and the ecstasy, of each nation. A great writer can portray events, people, with beauty and meaning, so that human experience is dignified and given a significance. People can learn from literature how to live and how to avoid the mistakes of other nations. Solzhenitsyn adds that in Russia, only the writer can really and effectively criticise the political rulers of the country: he can counteract the 'lie' – 'One word of truth is of more weight than all the rest of the world.'[14] Solzhenitsyn develops this theme much more fully in his most complete manifesto to date, namely 'Live not by lies', which is discussed in the next chapter.

Many people in the West have misunderstood these comments. For example, some people have objected to the charge that trade union activity is apparently a form of 'cave man impulse'. Others have suggested that Solzhenitsyn is too ready to take the sins of the world upon his shoulders, which is either much too daunting or else just a form of self-importance. Still others may argue that Solzhenitsyn attributes too much importance to the writer. In the television-dominated West, many seem to be arguing that there simply *must* be other means of achieving political opposition in the USSR.

Solzhenitsyn himself has said that his Nobel Prize speech failed to make a substantial impact on either the West or Russia. He says ruefully that 'over there, and here, they preferred not to understand it'.[15] He says that his meaning should have been clear enough from the speech itself; but it seems to me that he has explained his ideas on these matters much more clearly in one of his essays which has appeared in the collection *From Under the Rubble*. This essay is entitled 'Repentance and self-limitation'.

The essay is a remarkable attempt to reduce political and economic factors to more fundamental causes, which Solzhenitsyn sees as psychological and moral. For example, he sees inflation in the West as a product of psychology (the struggle for economic equality(?), lack of self-restraint) and the prevailing (materialistic) world outlook (from a press conference to explain the collection *From Under the Rubble*[16]). Thus he does not criticise (for example) the activities of trade unions and collective bargaining *as such*, but he attacks the motives involved. And these motives, in particular lack of 'self-limitation', he condemns universally. Not only trade unions are criticised. He points out that it was in reply to the 'shamelessness of unlimited money-grubbing that socialism in all its forms developed'.[17] So he is saying that at all stages of history there has been a general failure to practise self-limitation. Self-limitation is a particularly unpopular idea among nations, trade unions and political parties, except perhaps in extreme emergencies, when rationing for example became necessary and (in fact) beneficial. Solzhenitsyn argues here that political reform must today begin with reform of people. This is fundamental to his political outlook. Although this may seem to be a difficult task, time is short. Solzhenitsyn thinks that the idea of unlimited economic growth and technological progress must soon be seen to be self-defeating. This will lead to exhaustion of natural resources, conflict over resources and a ruined environment. We need instead to concentrate on *inward* development rather than outward development.

> After the Western ideal of unlimited freedom, after the Marxist concept of freedom as acceptance of the yoke of necessity – here is the true Christian definition of freedom. Freedom is self-restriction! Restriction of the self for the sake of others![18]

Obviously a moral revolution would be required to achieve this, and this is perhaps why Solzhenitsyn is so insistent upon the necessity for Christianity as an ideological basis for our social life. It should be noted in this context that Christianity has been officially disapproved and often actively persecuted in Russia and the USSR for nearly sixty years.

Self-limitation is necessary too if we are to preserve private property and our type of basically free-enterprise economy.

> No incentive to self-limitation has ever existed in bourgeois economics. . . . The fundamental concepts [however] of private property and private economic initiative are part of man's nature and necessary for his personal freedom and his sense of normal well-being[19]

– if only supporters of those ideas could limit themselves. He believes that nations too must practise self-limitation in their international dealings, not just for the sake of mankind as a whole but for their own well-being.

Does Solzhenitsyn lay too much emphasis on the moral responsibility of the writer? In the same essay ('Repentance and self-limitation') he goes even further, laying the guilt of nations at the feet of every individual citizen. In what way can it be said that a whole nation is guilty? And how can individuals, as members of those nations, be held responsible? If responsible, how may they repent and atone for what has been done?

Dealing with the first question, Solzhenitsyn suggests that it is natural to apply the moral concepts of individual life to social groups and nations. Like the individual, a nation, he argues, has a personality of its own which is mutable, changing. Like a person, a nation may sometimes do good and sometimes evil things. Like the individual it is bound to be guilty at times. British, French and Dutch colonialism, for instance, were sinful. Generally the populations of those countries participated in these adventures. Even in a totalitarian state, where the actions of government are not closely related to public opinion, people are responsible for what the state does; and in practice we often pay for those actions, even if they were carried out in the distant past. Some individuals (such as writers) may (and should) take it upon themselves to express repentance on behalf of their nation. If so, they are usually unpopular. But it can happen that a whole group of people in a nation feels repentant. For example, the intelligentsia as a social stratum in nineteenth-century Russia seemed to feel guilty towards the 'people'. Writers have a particularly important role in Russia as opinion-formers; for other forms of institutionalised dissent are weak or non-existent.

A nation can repent by deeds. Solzhenitsyn gives the example of West Germany, and suggests that former Chancellor Willy Brandt's policies towards Israel and his 'Ostpolitik' are examples of repentant policies, not dictated entirely by self-interest. Russia, too, can repent: indeed Solzhenitsyn argues that it is a national characteristic. However, in the twentieth century Russians have lost this art of repentance, and tended instead to take the most normal way out – namely, blaming other people, such as White Guards, kulaks, priests, sub-kulaks, wreckers, and so on (some of whose crimes were imaginary). He notes that whereas many other nations have perpetrated evil deeds abroad, a Russian characteristic has been to ill-treat its own people. The 'slimy swamp'[20] of Russian society is formed by Russians themselves. Surely, for example, there must have been at least a million people – guards, sadists, informers, betrayers – who made the Gulag Archipelago possible? If Russians want to make a new start, overcome the burden of the past, they themselves must repent. This helps to answer the question of *how*, in what way, the individual is supposed to atone for his actions. Repentance, of course, is always extremely painful. But Solzhenitsyn argues that this is what is required of a true patriot. National bolshevism (see Conclusion) is not therefore true patriotism. Moreover, repentance, if it is to be genuine, must be self-inclusive. It is no good blaming others, or trends in national thought, such as the idea of Moscow as the 'Third Rome', which for example is attacked by a group of writers in *Vestnik RSKhD* No. 97.[21] Repentance for the individual will be personally painful, intellectually difficult, socially unpopular, and one is likely to be accompanied by some very doubtful fellow travellers. In the sphere of international relations, repentance is just as difficult and equally necessary. It must also be backed up with actions. For example, 'With regard to all the peoples in and beyond our borders forcibly drawn into our orbit, we can fully purge our guilt by giving them genuine freedom to decide their future for themselves.'[22] There should also be a greater readiness to renounce the use of force in international affairs.

Solzhenitsyn is clearly making some very radical demands, the most radical being that morality must begin to dictate the external and internal politics of nations. In one sense, this view may be seen as the antithesis of Machiavelli; and many people might be tempted to argue therefore that Solzhenitsyn has failed in some sense to understand the nature of politics. A closely allied criticism of Solzhenitsyn is that he is too ready to equate Marxism–Leninism with the Soviet experience. In the Nobel Prize speech, Solzhenitsyn certainly makes some startling comments about Marxism. It is an illusion, says Solzhenitsyn to suppose that any political ideology based on class struggle, or divisive creeds of any kind, can lead to a better, more humane world. So Marxism–Leninism is seen here as something which proves to be the antithesis of humanism. This view is quite the reverse of that held by a large body of Western opinion, which sees Marxism as profoundly humanistic in its ultimate aims and blessed with a very respectable intellectual pedigree. Solzhenitsyn would surely argue that this is a form of intellectual self-delusion, possible only in countries which have never experienced a Marxist regime. He goes ever further in the Nobel Prize speech, claiming that Marxism is particularly weak in the field of ethics, capable of using any means to achieve 'proletarian' revolution. This attitude, he claims, has led to a dangerously a-historical perspective, a lack of respect for traditional values and national differences, political amoralism and terrorist methods. These factors in their turn will always tend to undermine human society. He goes on to suggest that the original ideals of Marxism–Leninism can easily disappear as a result of the methods used to achieve the aims of a revolution, so that such a revolution will always tend to degenerate into an unfree, degenerate, terrorised society. He thus equates Marxist revolutionaries with Dostoevskii's 'Devils',[23] illustrated by the career of the horrible Peter Verkhovenskii in Dostoevskii's novel. Solzhenitsyn argues that such trends are rampant in the modern world, especially among the younger generation, from the Komsomol youth who break up the Russian Orthodox 'Easter Procession'[24] to such movements (perhaps he is saying) as 'Black September' for the liberation of Palestine. In making this assertion, Solzhenitsyn is of course echoing the conclusions of the authors of the collection *Iz glubiny*, which appeared in Moscow in 1918. The title of the new collection, *Iz pod glyb*, dealt with in this chapter and chapter 11 is obviously also an echo of the original.

These conclusions are extremely radical and startling to the Western reader, and they may seem absurdly oversimplified and unsubtle to Western Marxists. However, I do not think that we should for this reason dismiss Solzhenitsyn's ideas as confused or unrealistic. Solzhenitsyn is trying to explain and to warn: 'After all, we still have to explain the emergence of the "Gulag Archipelago"!'

The aim of this chapter has been to clarify some of Solzhenitsyn's more difficult ideas, contained in the Nobel Prize speech and in one essay from the collection *From Under the Rubble*. As before, my plea is simply that we should be clear about what is being said; and we should beware of making hasty judgements based on the traditions of conventional Western political thought. Solzhenitsyn is writing within a particular environment and his intellectual affinities are with a branch of nineteenth- and twentieth-century Russian political thought which is little known to educated opinion in the West.

Finally I want to deal with a criticism of Solzhenitsyn which has emerged not only in connection with the Nobel Prize speech. This criticism is related not so much to the content of Solzhenitsyn's remarks but to his tone of voice. Put simply, the criticism says that Solzhenitsyn is excessively dogmatic, even desperate, that he is too apt to express himself with exclamation marks and capital letters. For those of us who do not know or understand what it is like to live and work in the Soviet Union, let me try to explain. It is a formidable undertaking for one man, or even a smallish group of like-minded people, to oppose the might of the Soviet state. There have been times in Solzhenitsyn's career, especially after the demise of Khrushchev and in 1965 after the seizure of his archive by the KGB,[25] when Solzhenitsyn's beliefs, and even perhaps his Christian faith, may have seemed less than certain, less than secure. Like Tolstoi before him, Solzhenitsyn the moral, literary and intellectual giant has nevertheless stood almost alone against his society, the powers that be, prevailing trends in modern so-called civilisation. His supporters abroad were not always by any means people he could approve of, whose crude equation of Solzhenitsyn with any kind of anti-Sovietism he did not solicit or condone. In these circumstances we should not, I think, criticise Solzhenitsyn for adopt-ing a tone which sometimes seems rigid, inflexible or desperate. His fate has not been to debate the niceties of political theory or aesthetics in the easy liberal atmosphere of an English university: rather it has been to forge a coherent philosophy of life from harsh experience of living, persecution, perpetual political opposition, amidst largely un-comprehending and trivial world-wide attention. We should concen-trate, then, less upon the tone of voice in which Solzhenitsyn speaks and more on the content and subtle nature of what he is saying.

SUMMARY

Solzhenitsyn's philosophy of art, as expressed in his Nobel Prize speech, is important in understanding his political thought, because like Dostoevskii he elevates moral and aesthetic considerations above politi-cal ones. Moral considerations, not political programmes, should dictate one's social action according to the (infallible) guidance of one's conscience. The Nobel Prize speech proposes that in today's world, universal standards of justice must be discovered and ethical relativism must be abandoned. At the same time, Solzhenitsyn advocates that the rights of national self-determination and national development must be preserved. He believes that cosmopolitan internationalism lies in the distant future of mankind; but in the immediate future it is the role of the writer to preserve his nation's integrity and standards, as well as to create something lasting and educative for the human race, and to tell the truth in a way which neither political ideology nor any science is able to do.

    The essay 'Repentance and self-limitation' attempts to reduce political and economic phenomena to more fundamental, moral and psychological ones. Hence political reform must begin with the reform of people. Solzhenitsyn believes that Christianity is essential in this respect. and he proclaims the beneficial effects of genuine repentance and admission of guilt as a basis for a better future, both in the life of individuals and in the life of nations. He also proclaims the startling proposition that the principles of self-limitation and morality are essential to national and international politics, and he rejects Marxism in all its forms as socially divisive, saying that it is likely to lead to terrorism; and that if it is successful, it will create an inhuman society without an ethical basis.

NOTES

1   *Nobel Prize Lecture*, Stenvalley Press (1973), p. 13.
2   *Ibid.*
3   S. E. Finer, *Comparative Government*, Pelican (1970), p. 33.
4   *Nobel Prize Lecture*, *op. cit.*, p. 27.
5   *Ibid.*
6   E.g. Alan Myers, in *Solzhenitsyn in Exile*, Pathfinder Press, New York (1974), equates Solzhenitsyn's views with 'Great Russian nationalism' (p. 4).
7   *Nobel Prize Lecture*, *op. cit.*, p. 33. The Russian text is: 'tait v sebye osobuyu gran' Bozh'ego zamysla'.
8   H. Marcuse, *One-Dimensional Man*, Beacon Press (1964).
9   *From Under the Rubble*, Collins/Harvill (1975), p. 262.
10   *Nobel Prize Lecture*, *op. cit.*, p. 31.
11   *Ibid.*, p. 37.
12   *Ibid.*, p. 45.
13   *Ibid.*
14   *Ibid.*, p. 55.
15   *Bodalsya telyonok s dubom*, YMCA, Paris (1975), p. 360.
16   *Dve Press-Konferentsii (k sborniku 'Iz-pod glyb')*, YMCA, Paris (1975), p. 61.
17   *From Under the Rubble*, *op. cit.*, p. 138.
18   *Ibid.*, p. 136.
19   *Ibid.*, p. 138.
20   *Ibid.*, p. 118.
21   E.g. V. Gorskii, *Vestnik Russkogo studencheskogo christianskhogo dvizheniya*, No. 97, III (1970), pp. 33–68.
22   *From Under the Rubble*, *op. cit.*, p. 135.
23   *Nobel Prize Lecture*, *op. cit.*, p. 37.
24   A. Solzhenitsyn, *Stories and Prose Poems*, Bodley Head (1971), p. 126.
25   *Bodalsya telyonok s dubom*, *op. cit.*, p. 118.

11 Letter to Soviet leaders, as breathing and consciousness return: Advice to the Soviet people, 'Do not live by lies'

The content of Solzhenitsyn's explicit political programme – for that is what it is – appeared first in his 'Letter to Soviet Leaders', which was sent in September 1973 and published in Russian in the West in February 1974. In the same month, the most explicit moral and political injunction 'Live not by lies' appeared. Both of these statements have been further clarified and enlarged by Solzhenitsyn's remaining two essays in *From Under the Rubble*.

Solzhenitsyn's first point is that his letter must of necessity be a great rarity in the Soviet Union, because since everyone is a state employee or concerned about a party career, then any independent comment or criticism must be difficult to come by, and most advice to one's superiors must tend to be dominated by careerist calculations. This in itself is a feature tending towards despotism and sychophancy.

Solzhenitsyn, however, writes the Letter because he is profoundly concerned about the fate of his own country; he believes that Russia as an historical entity and as a nation is threatened. In effect he reads the Soviet leaders a kind of fatherly lecture, based on the supposition 'that you are not alien to your origins, to your fathers, grandfathers, and great-great-grandfathers'.[1] In accordance with the general line taken by the 'native soil movement' in the nineteenth century, and those who stood as it were between East and West, Solzhenitsyn associates Russia with Western civilisation and sees Russia threatened, in this role among others, by the People's Republic of China. Indeed, in some ways Russia is the strongest representative of Western culture today, says Solzhenitsyn, because the countries of Western Europe and the United States of America have become weakened, effete, lacking in self-confidence and moral strength, beset by crisis. In an interesting aside, he attributes this weakness not only to the effects of World War but also to 'historical, psychological and moral crisis affecting the entire culture and world outlook which were conceived at the time of the Renaissance and attained the acme of their expression with the eighteenth-century Enlightenment'.[2] (In a later passage, however, he remarks that Western Europe and the USA do still have an enormous capacity for adaptation, change and facing of challenge which the Soviet Union may lack.)

Solzhenitsyn points out that the present enormous strength and influence of the Soviet Union is not in fact due to its skill in diplomacy, which has often produced some very counter-productive results. He cites the aid given to the German Wehrmacht in the 1920s; the Nazi–Soviet pact; and subsequently, the aid and loans to Mao-Tse Tung. These represent failures of diplomacy and can be attributed to a misguided adherence to Marxism–Leninism, which advocates the fostering of revolution abroad by any means. In later articles and speeches (see chapter 13), Solzhenitsyn attributes Soviet power in the international sphere almost entirely to Western weakness and mistakes.

Solzhenitsyn suggests that the foreign policy of the USSR is not only dangerous and immoral but far too expensive and wasteful of national resources. In the collection *From Under the Rubble*, Solzhenitsyn points out that the Soviet Union conducts 37·5 per cent of total world arms trade.[3] Defence expenditure, says Solzhenitsyn, should be directed towards self-defence, particularly against China. In a war against China, Solzhenitsyn predicts that Russian casualties might be no less than 60 million. This loss would represent the effective 'extirpation' of the Russian people. Moreover Solzhenitsyn points out that such a war would in effect be seen, not as an ideological war, but a war of national defence. Few Russians would see their sacrifice as defence of Marxism or the revolution. 'Surely only the very, very first of them will die for that . . . [the correct interpretation of Lenin].'[4] In practice the emphasis in any such war will be placed on patriotism, defence of the Fatherland, and Orthodoxy, as in the Great Patriotic War. Solzhenitsyn suggests that if this conclusion is correct, then it shows that Marxism is effectively a dead ideology and that the building-up of patriotic feelings among the population is far more vital than political indoctrination. He points to the lack of patriotism among American troops in Vietnam, and their consequent loss of morale; and he warns against such decadence on the part of Russians. As far as ideology goes, Solzhenitsyn is not just critical, he is dismissive: 'Give them [the Chinese] their ideology. . . . The murky whirlwind of "progressive ideology" swept in on us from the West at the end of the last century – and has tormented and ravaged our soul quite enough.'[5] Solzhenitsyn's rejection of Marxism–Leninism is total, but he does not underestimate its power. At the Zürich press conference (16 November 1974), in answer to a crucial question from the Associated Press (part of which, in effect, was – how long will the regime last?), Solzhenitsyn said that Marxism was very far from dead in the Soviet Union. It motivated those in power, albeit in a crude and oversimplified form; it had been responsible for endless betrayals and false confessions in the 1930s (as it had done more recently in China as well); it had demanded that people surrender their 'soul', in that it forced people to act against their best friends and against their common sense (for example, a Marxist analysis accuses capitalism of being responsible for world starvation; why then does the Soviet Union need to import grain?). Only an ideology which proclaimed that the CPSU and its leader had discovered the laws of social development could have allowed Stalin to emerge to undisputed power; Lenin's fanatical hostility to the church was also based on ideology; and finally, the perversion which was the Gulag Archipelago could only have been possible because ideology had gripped the minds of its creators and its staff. The crucial point, however, is that Marxism has lost the support of Russian society.[6] Hence he is able to say without inconsistency, 'Take away this ideology and nothing will even collapse, nothing will even wobble.'[7]

Of course, Solzhenitsyn is ready to concede that one argument for ideology is the retention and legitimacy of power on the part of the party and the present rulers. Without the 'political formula' of Marxism–Leninism, it is difficult to see how the Communist Party of the Soviet Union could retain its political monopoly in the long term. Solzhenitsyn must realise this; but he does not think that the party's power is threatened in the short term. In the long term, he clearly believes that the best type of government for Russia is an authoritarian national government without political parties. In an essay devoted to a critique of Sakharov, which appears in *From Under the Rubble*, he begins by suggesting that intellectual freedom is of 'conditional, not intrinsic worth'.[8] The West has plenty of intellectual freedom but it is degenerate; also it has political freedom and in general practises multi-party parliamentarianism. Solzhenitsyn regards this form of government as a desirable ideal, but in practice corrupt and unstable in most countries, although he thinks that England might be an exception to the general rule and that politically advanced countries might eventually achieve the heights of stable democracy.[9] He believes that multi-party democracy would fail in Russia, just as it failed so quickly, signally and miserably after February 1917 in the period of Provisional Government. This form of government failed, among other reasons, for sheer lack of practice. After nearly sixty years of authoritarian rule, Russia would be even less ready for democracy. He believes that authoritarian rule is natural to Russia, and in a profound comment on authority and freedom he writes:

Freedom is moral: but only if it keeps within certain bounds, beyond which it degenerates into complacency and licentiousness. Order is not immoral, if it means a calm and stable system. But order too has its limits, beyond which it degenerates into arbitrariness and tyranny.[10]

In the essay cited above, he goes on to ask, some would say cryptically and enigmatically, 'Are there no *extraparty* or strictly *nonparty* paths of national development?'[11]

Perhaps this is a long-term desired aim for Solzhenitsyn; and in the 'Letter to Soviet Leaders' he suggests certain possible short-term changes. Like Shipov and the Octobrists, Solzhenitsyn places emphasis on the modification of the autocracy which might become possible through local government. He refers of course to the soviets (councils) which in 1905, and again in 1917–18, seemed to emerge naturally as democratic organs of workers, peasants and soldiers with some autonomy up to 6 July 1918.[12] Within the soviets he wants what he calls the 'widest possible consultation with all the working people'.[13] However he seems not to discuss the crucial issue of how this discussion and consultation can be limited. Consultation, participation and political power are all intimately connected, but Solzhenitsyn seems to believe that the party's effective monopoly of power need not be affected. Once again, it seems to me that he is talking about the short term as opposed to the long term. In a similar vein he advocates that people who are not necessarily party members should be allowed to rise to high positions within the state apparatus, and he suggests that these new powers for the soviets and for non-party delegates should be written into a new constitution. He does not at this stage try to challenge the powers of the party to supervise and check all aspects of government.[14] But he declares his opposition to the Stalinist 'hard line' administration, stressing that party authoritarianism must be a benevolent dictatorship.

Moreover, Solzhenitsyn demands that any government must be a *legal* government. We have shown above that he regards Stalin's system and Lenin's legacy as inherently arbitrary and illegal. For many years now, the official Soviet press has contained articles stressing that all 'administrative arbitrariness'[15] is inadmissible and dangerous. But Solzhenitsyn insists that a legal regime must have at least an independent judiciary, if not complete separation of powers. It is difficult to see how such a proposal is consistent with a thoroughgoing authoritarianism. As I have outlined above, it seems to me that Solzhenitsyn is advocating not so much a 'rule of law' in the full meaning of Professor Dicey, but rather a form of *Rechtstaat*.[16] Solzhenitsyn regards as possible a legal, benevolent, national and non-party authoritarianism in Russia.

Such an authoritarian regime would, he thinks, be acceptable to the Russian public, provided that it did not try to base its power on dishonest or shaky ideological foundations. In this context he calls for the *disestablishment* of Marxism, and its replacement by freedoms of political thought (including Marxism), religion, art, literature and publication. In his foreword to the collection *From Under the Rubble*, Solzhenitsyn argues that suppression of thought leads to 'distortion, ignorance and mutual incomprehension among compatriots and contemporaries'.[17] Thus it is that contemporary events and past history rapidly become unintelligible, a pile of rubble. We already know that Solzhenitsyn is opposed to any form of censorship.[18] But is genuine freedom of thought, particularly freedom of political thought, compatible with an authoritarian regime? Solzhenitsyn has this to say about authoritarian regimes:

> Authoritarian regimes as such are not frightening – only those which are answerable to no-one and nothing. The autocrats of earlier, religious ages, though their power was ostensibly unlimited, felt themselves responsible before God and their consciences.[19]

Some people might interpret this comment to mean that Solzhenitsyn is advocating a return to autocracy in Russia, and they might well point out that under Tsarism there was usually a considerable degree of censorship. Others would insist that it is not enough to rely upon the autocrat's feelings of responsibility before God and so on: what is needed is a *de facto* system of institutional checks and balances to protect people's rights. This immediately begins to look a little like the dreaded liberal democracy, which Solzhenitsyn seems to regard as inapplicable to Russia. In fact, however, Solzhenitsyn is quite consistent here, because he is insistent upon the primacy of a *moral*, personal revolution: freedom of thought must be exercised with 'self-limitation'. Likewise governments must exercise their powers in the same spirit. This may sound slightly unlikely, and I think Solzhenitsyn would be the first to admit this; but it is not in itself inconsistent. Nor is it totally impossible. If freedom of thought is incompatible with stable, powerful government, then surely (for example) the basis of our own democracy is threatened? Finally, it is nowhere stated in Solzhenitsyn's writings that he supports a return to Tsarist autocracy, although he suggests that it should have been more stoutly defended at the time and allowed to evolve more naturally, perhaps along the lines suggested by Shipov and the Octobrists. He does believe, however, that the ideological basis of Tsarism was less objectionable than Marxism–Leninism. One advantage of Tsarism was that it did not demand the totalitarian surrender of personal belief and integrity. These things are a matter for the individual, his own conscience, and God. It is permissible for a political regime to demand of the citizen 'those things which are

Caesar's'. However, if Caesar demands those things which are God's, that is a sacrifice which we 'dare not make'.

Marxism–Leninism is criticised on other grounds as well. As a theory of industrialisation, ownership and control, Marxism–Leninism is criticised on the unusual grounds that its whole emphasis on speedy industrialisation must lead, as under capitalism, to exhaustion of the earth's limited resources. Solzhenitsyn has powerful allies in this contention in the form of the Teilhard de Chardin society and the Club of Rome. Solzhenitsyn argues that both the Western bourgeois industrial path and the Marxist path of development must lead to a technological, or at least to a resources impasse, and that it is misguided of economists to place their emphasis on theories of 'convergence' between the two systems, since what is required is the 'total renewal and reconstruction of both East and West'.[20] Solzhenitsyn demands that the debates about Russia's correct path of economic development, famous in the last decades of the nineteenth century, should be reopened. However, he is not referring so much to the 'Controversy over capitalism',[21] but to the earlier contentions of the Slavophiles in respect of the economic future of the Russian Mir. It would be incorrect to name Solzhenitsyn as 'populist' in this respect.

Although Solzhenitsyn's economic ideas are not perhaps yet fully developed, it is clear that he is advocating a policy of national retrenchment and reform – in particular development of the Soviet north-east and the national exploitation of resources, with an accent on small-scale enterprise and advanced technology. As we saw earlier, he advocates also a large-scale withdrawal from foreign aid programmes, especially expenditure on arms for foreign revolutionaries, who might not after all thank the Soviet Union for this expenditure anyway (Egypt?). Once again this requires rejection of Marxism and Leninism and the renouncing of world revolution as a policy aim. Solzhenitsyn claims also that rejection of Marxism–Leninism would lead to greater *consistency* in Soviet foreign policy. Marxism–Leninism preaches revolution by any available means, and for this reason Soviet policy has followed a rather opportunistic course,[22] while at the same time trying to justify its actions in terms of ideology. This has created cynicism and bewilderment among Soviet people. Solzhenitsyn is asking Soviet leaders to be consistent and open about the USSR's real national interests, and to interpret those interests with realism.

Solzhenitsyn also levels a series of very searching criticisms against Soviet internal policy, including the suggestion that conscription should be ended and that army education should be humanised, along with certain improvements in the state system and greater prestige and pay for teachers. He advocates greater care in town planning, with fewer cars in town centres and an end to high-rise flats. He criticises very strongly the apparent widespread alcoholism in Russian life; and he suggests that both work-loads and a noisy environment may be partly to blame. He criticises the destruction of the Russian countryside perpetrated by heavy machinery and industrial effluent. He believes that the economy and cultural life of the country are too centralised, and that as a result the majority of Russian cities other than Moscow and Leningrad are depressing and provincial. Similarly the capital cities are themselves overburdened and losing their character. He is especially depressed by the sordid living conditions of families in the big cities, and bemoans the illiterate trivialisation of working-class life. He is particularly concerned about the fate of children in Russia, and suggests that women should not be forced by economic circumstances (their husband's low wages) to take jobs. He believes that women should be able to look after their children, and does not equate women's rights with universal female employment on a par with men. Above all he deplores the assignment of women to heavy labour, believing this to be a form of oppression rather than women's liberation. Once again, it is necessary to clarify Solzhenitsyn's views here. He is *not* opposed to the idea of equal rights for women. He is saying, (a) that women should be able to *choose* whether to work or not – they should not be forced to work by economic considerations; (b) that children have rights as well – women with children should acknowledge these rights; and (c) that the spectacle of women employed in heavy labour, such as manual labour on building sites or railways, is indicative of a barbaric society.[23]

How, then, are these radical changes to be achieved? First and foremost, Solzhenitsyn rejects any ideas of physical or political revolution. In his first essay in the collection *From Under the Rubble*, Solzhenitsyn writes: 'No, let us not wish either "revolution" or "counter-revolution" on our worst enemies.'[24] At the press conference of 16 November 1974 Solzhenitsyn was asked by a German correspondent whether his proposals would not lead to new blood-letting in the Soviet Union. In answer to this question, Solzhenitsyn defined the difference between 'physical revolution' and 'moral revolution'. He said that the former always required violence in the hope of achieving justice, whereas it normally led to an escalation of violence. The latter required a willingness to sacrifice oneself, and if necessary to die, but not to kill others. In this way one remains consistent to one's beliefs, and may prove them attractive to others. Instead of physical revolution, Solzhenitsyn is advocating a kind of civil disobedience or passive resistance.[25]

Once again, we in the West can easily fail to understand the significance of this proposal, Social life in the Soviet Union requires its citizens not to be silent and acquiescent but to *participate*, especially if they are members of the party or intelligentsia. Commentators on the Soviet scene, such as Professor L. G. Churchward, have become enthusiastic about the apparent extent of citizen participation in public life.[26] Soviet citizens are obliged to vote in elections to the Soviets, for which there are direct elections at all levels. Hence all Soviet citizens vote more often than electors in Britain. Moreover the electors, under general guidance from the party, are responsible for their own electoral registration, and the electoral wards are smaller than in Britain. The Soviets thus contain a very large number of delegates, who are often well known to their electors. The executive committees of the Soviets carry out the functions of local government, and there is no body of permanent paid officials comparable to the local government officers in Britain. About 10 per cent of the eligible age group in the USSR are party members, and these are responsible for a wide range of tasks within their Primary Party Units including supervision of the economy and political education in all factories, schools, departments and other social organisations.* Perhaps one third of the eligible age group are members of the Young Communists or Komsomol. An even greater proportion of schoolchildren participate in the junior organisations of the party, the Octobrists and the Pioneers. Finally, under Khrushchev, citizens were required to take part in voluntary work under the general direction of the Soviets. This looks like an extremely formidable method of political socialisation, but is it, in fact, genuine participation?

Firstly, only one candidate stands in the elections. That candidate is pre-selected by the party and is either a party member or someone approved by the party. Voting is not effectively secret, since an unmarked paper deposited in the public ballot box is counted as a positive vote. Entry into the polling booth is therefore a conspicuous act. One may doubt whether the process of electoral registration is genuine political participation. Finally, the Soviet itself usually operates from the same building as the local party organisation, and is effectively controlled and supervised by that party organisation. Party discussions and elections are not secret, and elections to party posts are indirect,[27] being controlled from above by a department of the secretariat of the Central Committee. Since 1921, any 'fractionalism' or opposition groups within the party have been illegal. The principle of 'democratic centralism' (Rule 19 of the Party Rules) means that the decisions of higher bodies are binding upon lower party organisations. Trade unions are integrated into the state apparatus, and they are subordinate in practice to the party. Strikes are illegal.[28] Citizen participation in voluntary organisations within the Soviets and the 'comrades' courts' have greatly declined since the mid-sixties.

---

* Trade unions are now integrated into the state apparatus and their bargaining functions are subordinate to numerous state functions, including social security, safety, labour discipline and consultation with management and party about plan fulfilment. But membership is extremely pervasive.

The total result of this is that genuine democracy within the Soviets is very limited. The bicameral Supreme Soviet meets for only a few days of the year and always votes unanimously in both houses for legislation which is presented to it. Inner party democracy is virtually non-existent, and votes at party meetings are usually unanimous. Readers of the Soviet press (which is state-controlled) will know that party meetings, plena and congresses are invariably attended by delegates who applaud at the required moments according to well-known prescribed formulae, from '[applause]' to the less usual '[prolonged, loud applause, all stand]'. In the rare event of dissidence or deviation, the party 'machine' will arrange for condemnation to be published, both from groups of workers and peasants and from prominent citizens. Employment will be refused to friends and relatives of dissidents. This whole picture therefore represents not so much participation as *manipulation*.

Solzhenitsyn's suggestion is simply that the regime would be considerably weakened if a sufficiently large number of people openly refused to be manipulated. In his famous injunction, 'Live not by lies', he sets out specific proposals. He points out that this form of civil disobedience is much less dangerous than the form practised by followers of Gandhi against the British administration in India: it does not require positive action such as the impedance of public transport or any form of 'sit-in'. He asks simply that people should not *necessarily* applaud at public meetings; that they should not read the party or state-controlled press if they regard it as uninformative or untrue; that they should not, above all, sign defamatory letters against their colleagues simply because they are pressurised to do so. Some people have criticised Solzhenitsyn for his apparent dismissal of Marxism–Leninism as simply false: they have argued that one cannot easily apply the concepts of 'truth'/'falsehood (lies)' to political theory. It is, I think, true that Solzhenitsyn himself regards Marxism–Leninism as false; in the same way as he sees Christianity as incontrovertibly true. But Solzhenitsyn is not asking everyone to agree without any reservations with his own world outlook. He is saying quite simply that people must be true to themselves. Presumably under his proposals it would be possible for a Soviet communist to participate in all the required public actions if he believed that they were right and necessary. He asks only 'let us refuse to say what we do not think'.[29]

Even this course of action is dangerous in the Soviet Union. It may well result in the loss of one's job, the loss of one's Moscow residence permit, possibly even arrest or incarceration in a psychiatric institution. It could result in reprisals against one's family and friends, and above all it might result in academic failure of students, since all examinations in the Soviet Union carry compulsory papers on political economy,

party history, and so on, which require the 'approved' answers. However, Solzhenitsyn points out that it is very unlikely that there could
ever be a return to the Stalinist terror, when such actions might have
resulted in hard labour and death or execution in the Gulag Archipelago. Today, one would still be able to live, to have a roof over one's
head and some kind of basic living standards, even if this proves only
to be black bread and water for oneself and one's family. He believes
that this is the only way to keep one's self-respect and the respect of
one's children. And he points out that paper academic qualifications
are not the most important aim of education. He argues finally that if
the future belongs to anyone, it belongs to the younger generation, and
if they do not act, they cannot create a better society. This is quite
consistent with his belief that a better society can only be created by
the moral improvement of individuals.

He points out that such action is always painful at first, rather like
passing through a constricting filter or the 'eye of a needle', and that
each hole in the filter is only big enough to contain one person. But
later this path of action becomes easier. Here, he is no doubt relating to
his own experience, which he summarises in *The Oak and the Calf*, outlined in the introduction. He proposes, then, not so much a mass
movement as a series of isolated actions by individuals who, he suggests,
would soon come to recognise their community of interest with those
on the 'other side of the filter'. He hopes that this stream will become a
flood which, as he outlines in his essay *The Smatterers*, would consist not
only of the intelligentsia (defined as those with tertiary education) but
also of representatives of 'the people' as well, because the primary
qualities required are not intellectual but *moral*.[30] He compares such a
movement to the formation of crystals about a nucleus, and this could
become not so much a political movement or a social stratum but what
he calls a spiritual elite.[31] He hopes that the people involved might be
numbered in tens of thousands; and he suggests that positive action,
such as voluntary residence in and development of the Soviet north-
east, might then be required of them.

Solzhenitsyn points out that there are reasons to believe that such
action would be effective. 'Has not the great European nation Czechoslovakia – betrayed and deceived by us – demonstrated how even an
armourless breast, if it holds a worthy heart, can stand up to the on-
slaught of tanks?'[32] Referring to the apparent importance to the Soviet
regime of social manipulation, he explains why such action would be
so effective in Russia: 'because the LIE holds everything together, like
so many fasteners, several dozen to each man'.[33] Solzhenitsyn believes
that the time to act is now. In the first place he thinks that technology
may soon provide the regime with new methods of social control. 'If
we bow down even further and wait longer, our brothers the biologists

may then help to bring nearer the day when our thoughts can be read and our genes restructured.'[34] Moreover he believes that time is running out for the Russian nation, in the sense that present Soviet policies are extremely damaging. He estimates that the Soviet Union may have at most ten years (from 1973) to make the changes required. Every system, he says, either finds a way to develop or else collapses; and here we find a kind of Burkean echo: 'A state without the means of some change is without the means of its conservation.'[35] It is difficult to find any sort of scientific basis for Solzhenitsyn's time scale.

Similarly, he suggests, again without supporting arguments, that if a programme of civic disobedience of non-participation were to be launched, involving perhaps tens of thousands, 'this would change our country in MONTHS, not years'.[36] If, however, people fail to act, waiting for reform from above by the next generation, as Roy Medvedev suggests, or for changes over an even longer period by concentrating on cultural development,[37] then it will be too late. Finally he has this to say:

> If we are too frightened to do anything then we are a hopeless and worthless people and the contemptuous lines of Pushkin fit us well:
>
> What use to herds the gifts of freedom?
> The scourge, and a yoke of tinkling bells
> – this is their heritage, bequeathed to every generation.[38]

SUMMARY

Solzhenitsyn attributes the contemporary might and power of the Soviet Union, not to its international diplomacy, but to the weakness of the West. In fact the foreign policy of the USSR is based on false principles, says Solzhenitsyn, which are damaging to real national interests. Solzhenitsyn condemns excessive arms expenditure, saying that the only significant danger to the USSR today is China. In this context he advocates the diminution of Soviet commitments abroad and concentration on a policy of national retrenchment and reform, including the development of the Soviet north-east. He rejects the argument that Marxism is necessary to maintain the legitimacy of the regime, saying that if there were to be a war with China, it would not be an ideological war but a war of national defence like the Great Patriotic War. Solzhenitsyn believes that non-Party members should be allowed to stand for posts in the Soviets and in government, and that there should be greater democracy and freedom of speech within the Soviets, government and society. However, Solzhenitsyn maintains that such changes would not fundamentally alter the party's political monopoly or its authority, and he stresses that the Soviet Union is not yet ready for full democracy. Solzhenitsyn thus appears to believe that the CPSU can remain in power in the USSR without the ideological support of Marxism, and that a legal, benevolent and increasingly non-party authoritarianism could be possible.

If Solzhenitsyn's political views are unusual, his economics are also idiosyncratic in that he rejects not only Marxian socialism but also capitalism. He seems to advocate instead cooperative enterprise based on small-scale units with high technology and great emphasis on the revitalisation of agriculture, with more local autonomy and decentralisation. He hopes thus to improve working conditions, local community and family life, and the environment of town and country. It is not quite clear how such aims are compatible with authoritarian government.

In order to achieve his aims and to express opposition to the existing regime, he proposes a kind of civic or personal disobedience, which involves refusal to be manipulated into the enforced social participation which is a feature of Soviet life. He is not proposing any kind of political organisation for this purpose, but the spontaneous formation of a kind of spiritual elite who will recognise their community of interest and present insoluble problems for the totalitarian regime. He asks the young people of Russia to take special note of his programme 'Live not by lies', and suggests that they have a moral duty to act, even if their action means failure to pass exams or to advance their careers. The future of Russia belongs to its young people, he says, and if they do not act, they will have proved that they are fit only for servitude.

NOTES
1 'Letter to Soviet Leaders', Index on Censorship/Fontana (1974), pp. 7–8.
2 *Ibid.*, p. 12.
3 *From Under the Rubble*, Collins/Harvill (1975), p. 139n.
4 'Letter to Soviet Leaders', *op. cit.*, p. 17.
5 *Ibid.*, p. 18.
6 *Dve Press-Konferentsii*, YMCA, Paris (1975), p. 76.
7 'Letter to Soviet Leaders', *op. cit.*, p. 46.
8 *From Under the Rubble*, *op. cit.*, p. 18.
9 *Ibid.*, p. 19.
10 'Letter to Soviet Leaders', *op. cit.*, p. 51.
11 *From Under the Rubble*, *op. cit.*, p. 19.
12 'Letter to Soviet Leaders', *op. cit.*, p. 53.
13 *Ibid.*
14 *Ibid.*, p. 54.
15 *Administrativnyi proizvol'*.
16 See chapter 2. A *Rechtstaat* is defined historically by *Harrap's Standard German and English Dictionary* as 'A state in which governmental power is subject to the law' (Part 1, Vol. 3).
17 *From Under the Rubble*, *op. cit.*, foreword, p. ix.

18 A. Solzhenitsyn, 'Protest against expulsion from Union of Writers' (12 November 1969), in L. Labedz (ed.), *Solzhenitsyn – A Documentary Record*, 2nd edition, Pelican (1974), p. 224.
19 *From Under the Rubble, op. cit.*, pp. 23–4.
20 'Letter to Soviet Leaders', *op. cit.*, p. 21.
21 A. Walicki, *The Controversy over Capitalism*, Oxford: Clarendon Press (1969).
22 'Letter to Soviet Leaders', *op. cit.*, p. 58.
23 *Ibid.*, p. 40.
24 *From Under the Rubble, op. cit.*, p. 13.
25 *Ibid.*, p. 25.
26 L. G. Churchward, *Soviet Studies* (April 1966).
27 L. G. Churchward, *Contemporary Soviet Government*, Routledge & Kegan Paul (1975), p. 226.
28 M. Fainsod, *How Russia is Ruled*, Harvard (1970), p. 519.
29 A. Solzhenitsyn, 'Live not by lies', in L. Labedz (ed.), *op. cit.*, p. 377.
30 *From Under the Rubble, op. cit.*, p. 271.
31 *Ibid.*, p. 273.
32 'Live not by lies', *op. cit.*, p. 378.
33 *From Under the Rubble, op. cit.*, p. 275.
34 'Live not by lies', *op. cit.*, p. 379.
35 E. Burke, *Reflections on the Revolution in France*, Pelican (1968), p. 106.
36 *Dve Press-Konferentsii, op. cit.*, p. 81.
37 *Ibid.*
38 'Live not by lies', *op. cit.*, p. 379.

12 *Lenin in Zürich*

In the autumn of 1975, Solzhenitsyn published in Paris several chapters from his historical studies. These chapters were grouped together under the collective title of *Lenin in Zürich*. Solzhenitsyn's view of history seems to be that it is like a complex network, joined together by crucial concurrences of events and people, which he calls 'knots'. This analogy may possibly owe something to Pushkin. Already we have seen the first 'knot', *August 1914*; and two others, *October 1916* and *March 1917* are to appear shortly. *Lenin in Zürich* represents chapters from all three knots. From the invaluable personal record *The Oak and the Calf*, we know two facts which are important here. First, Solzhenitsyn plans no fewer than twenty such knots,[1] which make up surely one of the most ambitious literary projects of our time. Second, we know that from at least the early sixties Solzhenitsyn saw his work as a 'literary conspiracy'.[2] designed to enlighten the Russian public by a carefully planned programme of publication at home. However, publication in the Soviet Union required the approval of censorship, so Solzhenitsyn had to leave out some of the more uncompromising chapters, for example from *The First Circle*,[3] and one from *August 1914*. In these chapters, therefore, we get a particularly clear idea of Solzhenitsyn's political views, and it is both interesting and crucial to understand Solzhenitsyn's attitude towards Lenin.

In the first place there is no doubt that Solzhenitsyn is well versed in the available historical evidence about Lenin during the period of the First World War. From the works of Lenin himself, and from some important German sources which he lists,[4] Solzhenitsyn tries to reconstruct a picture of Lenin as a man, his personal motivations, his fanatical dedication to revolution, his relations with other social democrats, the changing tides of his fortunes and moods, and Solzhenitsyn sheds new light on the complex negotiations which took place over a period of time between Lenin and German representatives. Thus, whereas the present official Soviet one-volume party history (1969)[5] deals only with the development of Lenin's Marxist theory during this period, ending with the cryptic comment, 'On 3 April [1917] V. I. Lenin arrived in Petrograd',[6] we now have a new perspective on Lenin's life between 1914 and 1917, and a little new information as to how Lenin managed to arrive at the Finland station on the above date. And while we in the West gain just a few new insights, Russians who read Solzhenitsyn's account are sure to be shaken and startled.

Two criticisms of Solzhenitsyn are likely to recur in this context and elsewhere in his works. First, it might be said that he does not do justice to Lenin's overall historical prescience which some would see (despite Lenin's recorded moments of doubt) as largely correct. However, there is evidence here that Solzhenitsyn is well acquainted with Lenin's works, and Lenin's historical prescience is deeply questioned by Solzhenitsyn, who puts forward the alternative thesis that Lenin was himself wavering and doubtful about the possibilities of revolution in Russia, indeed almost despairing in the autumn of 1916, and that his ideas about the possibility of revolution in other countries were not so much improbable as wildly fantastic. Moreover the overall picture presented to us in *August 1914* and in this account of Lenin is that the war was a major factor weakening Tsarism from within, and that in this and other ways Lenin was not so much prescient as amazingly lucky.

A second possible line of criticism is that Solzhenitsyn's reconstructions of Lenin's life, conversations and thoughts are tendentious and biased. Solzhenitsyn sometimes adopts the Tolstoyan literary technique which may be termed psychological introspective analysis. Whereas in *War and Peace* Tolstoi attempted to reconstruct the mental processes of Napoleon after the battle of Borodino,[7] Solzhenitsyn has depicted Stalin in the late 1940s in his secret Kremlin apartment ('One night in the life of Stalin' in *The First Circle*). Similarly, here Lenin is shown as he walks the Zürich streets (now familiar to Solzhenitsyn), musing before the statue of Zwingli, at work in a Zürich library, and so on. Is it really possible for a historian to reconstruct such moments from available sources, photographic, written, printed and personal experience? While history remains, as largely it must, an art rather than a science, Solzhenitsyn's technique is surely both permissible and indispensable while his conclusions remain convincing. At the outbreak of war, Lenin in Cracow is seen as a man surprised by external events. Obsessed with his political struggles against fellow socialists, opposing the 'infection of unification',[8] he barely heard of the events leading up to war, just as he had been caught unawares by the 1905 revolution in Russia. Lenin's fellow socialists, however, were more generous than he, and the intervention of Polish and Austrian social democrats, Hanecki, V. Adler and Diamand, saved him from his initial Austrian imprisonment, while Hanecki helped him also financially. Here Lenin is shown as the political and financial realist before being socialist or idealist; and he is depicted as ungrateful in that these non-Bolsheviks were not only later cast aside but also viciously attacked. Solzhenitsyn remarks that Lenin had very few real friends; so many, Plekhanov, Martov, Valentinov, had proven disappointments to him. By 1914 the term 'friendship' was meaningless to this 'political genius'.[9]

Lenin, the professional politician, the leviathan who respected only great men and the mighty events of history, was full of 'joy'[10] at the outbreak of war, not only because it would weaken Tsarism but also because it would transfer the centre of gravity of Russian political opposition into emigration and because it put an end to any silly socialist pressures about the need for unification, since most Mensheviks and European social democrats had voted for War Credits. This account is at variance with some well-known Western accounts, such as Ulam, Wolfe and Payne,[11] who stress Lenin's initial shock and horror at the socialists' War Credit votes. Solzhenitsyn suggests at least that Lenin recovered very quickly.

In any case, Solzhenitsyn suggests that Lenin's mood as he travelled via Brussels to Switzerland would have been quite good, not only because of the outbreak of war but also because in Brussels Lenin would meet Inessa Armand, whose relationship with Lenin is seen as particularly important. Solzhenitsyn seems to be saying that Lenin compares favourably Inessa's fundamentally amoral outlook with the superficial and narrow moralism of many European social democrats. In this context Solzhenitsyn records Lenin's contempt for the moderate pacifist socialists, and says that Lenin greatly admired the mighty power of Imperial Germany as a much more important political force than pacifist socialism. Everyone, including the official Soviet party history, knows and spells out Lenin's idea, expressed in his 'Theses on War', of turning the European imperialist war into revolutionary civil wars in the belligerent countries. But here Solzhenitsyn points up the inconsistency of Lenin's position; for while in public he was strongly opposed to the war, at the same time he hoped privately that it would prolong itself in order to achieve its revolutionary aims.[12] Finally it remains obscure how Lenin imagined that German victory could lead on to a proletarian revolution.

In the sections from the 'knot' *October 1916* Solzhenitsyn opens with a scene at a restaurant in Zürich where members of the 'Skittle Club', social democrats such as Radek, Platten and others, are trying to grasp and apply this essentially difficult Leninist political line. In particular, the slogans adopted by Zimmerwald left,[13] such as 'Civil War', 'The era of the bayonet has come!', or the dictum that true revolutionaries never fear a split in their party, seemed inapplicable, along with the theses contained in *Imperialism, the Highest Stage of Capitalism*, to a country like Switzerland which was neutral and had no empire. Lenin however pointed out certain potentially revolutionary features in Swiss society: Switzerland was an essential financial centre of international capitalism, a 'republic of lackeys'. Moreover, since its armed forces took the form of armed militia, it would be relatively easy to arm the Swiss proletariat. Switzerland's democratic constitution would make subversion, such as proposals for disarmament, and general political organisation, simpler than in Russia or any other belligerent country. Finally, since Switzerland was a trilingual country at the heart of Europe, it could serve as a base for European revolution.[14]

The 'Skittle Club' members were intrigued by this analysis, and proposed to present a cautious resolution, about disarmament (with retention of militia arms) and the need for peaceful, European socialism, to the forthcoming congress of Swiss social democrats. With care, they succeeded in getting the motion adopted. While introducing the motion, Lenin was careful to say that he opposed the use of any terror (apropos the assassination by a social democrat of the prime minister of Austria–Hungary) if it were carried out on an opportunistic individual basis. Terror must be part of a political strategy, he said. The delegates, it seemed, failed to understand him, and voted for the motion. Solzhenitsyn remarks that this is how to move slowly (but surely) to the left.[15] The motion was later adopted by the youth movement as well, and was only reversed when Robert Grimm's *Berner Tagvacht* reported the foreign, suspicious, origins of the motion ('. . . certain foreigners, examining our workers' movement through their own eyes, and absolutely indifferent to Swiss affairs, want . . . to stir up our revolution.'[16]).

This episode depicts Lenin very clearly as a political intriguer and a Jacobin rather than a Marxist, willing to apply his techniques, including mass terror, to any society, more or less regardless of its objective social conditions and of Marxist theory.

At the same time, Lenin's need for the correct political formulae is not overlooked. Solzhenitsyn suggests that Lenin must have approved of the figure of Zwingli, whose statue stands in Zürich, holding a sword in one hand and a bible in the other. (The bible is understandable in the sixteenth century.) Lenin, says Solzhenitsyn, would have approved of the idea of a 'book extended by the sword'.[17] Lenin's approval of Clausewitz is also recorded: 'All politics leads to war,'[18] and other dicta.

Lenin is seen at this time to be in desperate financial straits. He planned to ask for money from Bonch-Bruevich or Gorkii, although at the same time bitterly attacking the 'Machists'[19] and Gorkii's circle. He admitted that Shlyapnikov could not spare any party funds from Russia, but Solzhenitsyn suggests that Lenin would have made use of these funds for his personal purposes if he could. Once again Lenin is depicted as calculating, ungrateful and unscrupulous; but not quite inhuman, since at least he was dependent on Inessa Armand. 'Inessa was the one person in the world on whom he felt, acknowledged, his dependence.'[20] At the same time Lenin was worried that Inessa was being unfaithful to him;

for not only had their relationship deteriorated since April after the Kienthal meeting, but also Inessa had always believed in 'free love'. He had argued against these theories: 'Her ill-defined theories about free love, totally unfounded on class-analysis . . . were surely refuted – but she remained free and unconquerable.'[21]

However, Lenin compared his wife Nadya (Krupskaya) unfavourably with Inessa. His wife was a great practical help to him, despite her illnesses, but she was totally subservient to him, agreeing with him in everything, and had become a kind of pale imitation of him. Is this perhaps a comment on Lenin's character? – the man who seeks, strives everywhere to be dominant, but in the end respects only those who remain free, treating inconsiderately those who become subservient?

Lenin's hatred of religion is here remarked upon as Lenin's typical work day in one of the Zürich libraries – a former church – is summarised. (Lenin, we are told, celebrated Zwingli's achievement in closing Catholic churches and turning them over to civic use. It gave Lenin 'especial pleasure that both chief libraries in Zürich triumphed over religion'.[22] Solzhenitsyn remarks on Lenin's amazing capacity for work, and at several subjects simultaneously. But at the same time he is seen as a monomaniac, totally intolerant of opposition and dedicated to his version of the socialist revolution. Socialism is only possible through revolution, civil war and dictatorship. Pacifism is absurd: even women and children of thirteen would be involved in the struggle. Moreover, although a democratic phase must accompany a socialist revolution, as Russian Marxists such as Bukharin had overlooked, this democracy must be squashed as soon as possible.[23]

During the course of his work, Lenin often reviewed the characters and reliability of the leading Bolsheviks: Shlyapnikov, Kollontai, Trotskii, Radek, Malinovsky. It seemed that he esteemed Malinovsky most highly of these, comparing his potential to that of the famous German socialist Bebel. Lenin refused to believe, even at this time, that Malinovsky was a provocateur. He himself had been only too pleased to confirm Malinovsky in the Central Committee of the party, together with the enigmatic Stalin, who had been put forward by Malinovsky.[24] Surely here, Solzhenitsyn is suggesting not only that Lenin might have been on crucial occasions a poor judge of character, but also that Stalin was himself tarred with Malinovsky's brush. (Hingley and others have suggested that Stalin at one time worked for the Okhrana.*)

The most important part of Lenin's daily work at this time was reading the papers and keeping in touch with the war news and political news. In particular, Lenin noted the fortunes of the Russian army, noting down their losses 'with pleasure and amazement'.[25] Lenin is depicted as heart-

* Tsarist secret police.

less and ruthless, interested only in events as factors contributing to his eventual political success. But while reading about these terrible losses, Lenin found in the end some cause for gloom. 'If they [the Russian peasantry] could endure such a war and not rise – what could be done with them?'[26] Lenin at this time seemed to go through a state of mind akin to depression. He concluded that there would be no revolution in Russia; and even worse, he became convinced that the Tsar was planning a separate peace with Germany. This would be a brilliant solution for the Tsar, 'exactly what Lenin would do in his place':[27] especially because he could see no reason why Germany, caught in stalemate battle on two fronts, should oppose the idea.

However, Lenin pulled himself together, and Solzhenitsyn puts words into Lenin's mouth which suggest that Solzhenitsyn sees politicians as less than human: 'In general, a politician is not someone who depends on age, feelings or circumstances, so much as one who at all times of the year and day is a reliable mechanism for action, speeches and struggle.'[28] Yet even the resilient, dedicated Lenin had his weak moments. Solzhenitsyn suggests that Lenin's health was poor at this time, and that he suffered from headaches, perhaps the early symptoms of cerebral haemorrhage which eventually killed him. His 47 years of struggle seemed to have borne no fruit; he was poor and in bad health. 'And that to which had been called, to influence the course of history, was not given to him.'[29] This account is a very sympathetic, and indeed empathetic, picture of Lenin's despair. Does Solzhenitsyn perhaps see *himself* as a figure of Lenin's stature and significance, a kind of anti-Lenin?

Lenin, it seems, was never a patriot, cursing his luck at having been born a Russian, so that alternative avenues of political activity were closed to him. He concluded that since a real socialist should be an internationalist, then the only future for him was to build the Third International on the lines laid down by the Zimmerwald left. He resolved to go to America, to join Bukharin and Trotskii, and in his despair he believed not only that Russia would conclude a separate peace but also that the Tsar would make some arrangement for constitutional monarchy in Russia with the Kadets, and there would be 20–30 years of bourgeois development with no need or opportunity of a revolution.[30] Solzhenitsyn says that he had actually put the idea of the trip (to America) to Krupskaya when suddenly there arrived from Berlin a German emissary, a mysterious individual already known to him through the social democrat Parvus: Georg Sklarz.

Sources in English seem to have little information about Georg Sklarz.[31] Solzhenitsyn however says that on this occasion, Sklarz handed Lenin a four-page letter from Parvus, a man greatly respected by Lenin, who saw him as a brilliant Marxist, one of the first to advocate the idea of using the Soviets as organs of government. In 1905, he

had acquitted himself in the St Petersburg Soviet with honour. Solzhenitsyn remarks that a crucial point (as far as Lenin was concerned)
what that although Parvus was not aligned at any time with the
Bolsheviks, he was never hostile to Lenin.

The interesting proposal contained in the letter was that Parvus
should come and discuss personally some urgent matters of mutual
interest. Lenin already knew the substance of Parvus's plans. Parvus's
reasoning was that since social democracy was strongest in Germany, if
Germany was defeated, then socialism 'would be beaten everywhere'.[32]
Moreover a German victory would be necessary in the end to crush
Tsarism. His slogan was, 'For democracy, against Tsarism'. As to what
might happen after a German victory, Lenin already knew that in theory,
Parvus-Helphand supported the thesis of transforming the war into civil
war. Workers' parties of the world, he suggested, should unite to fight
'against Russian Tsarism'.[33] He seemed to be at one with Lenin over the
point that the proletariat could not just remain neutral, as Trotski had
advocated. His fantastic plans for the subversion of the Russian empire[34]
included support for Ukrainian, Georgian and Armenian nationalists,
thus uniting the aims of socialism and nationalism in a way which (Solzhenitsyn suggests) might have appealed to Lenin. So also did the idea of
unleashing peasant uprisings, military insurrections, and so on, while
the fall of Tsarism would be hailed by the international socialist and
liberal press, gaining support from public opinion in the USA.[35] The
fall of Tsarism would allow publication of secret treaties exposing the
Entente. And in this fantastic, geopolitical plan, the Russian socialists
had an especially important role to play. These, however, were weak and
divided, though sections already supported Parvus's ideas – for example,
the Finnish Party and Jewish Bund. But Lenin above all was crucial;
and this opinion Parvus had already in 1916 conveyed in a memorandum
to the German government. His proposal was that if Lenin would
support the cause with the appropriate Bolshevik 'defeatist' slogans,
Parvus would obtain one million marks for Bolshevik funds, to be
followed by a further five million. He said also that Rakovskii, Trotskii
and Martov had received money. He even proposed to arrange the
beginning of the Russian revolution on 9 January 1917 (the anniversary
of 'Bloody Sunday', 1905).

Solzhenitsyn makes much of the interaction between Lenin and
Parvus, suggesting that they had at least three meetings, direct and indirect, between the beginning of 1916 and March 1917. He says that at
one point Lenin was quite taken with Parvus's massive plans for subversion, although at the same time repelled. 'Lenin was sickened by his
self assurance, but fascinated by the reality of his power.'[36] Lenin, says
Solzhenitsyn, was in complete agreement about the role of money as a
means to power, and that such opportunities come only once: 'Money is

power.'[37] 'In the highest centre of his thought Parvus was undoubtedly right.'[38] Lenin is shown here as greatly tempted by Parvus's offer, which appeared again through the medium of Sklarz at a critical juncture in Lenin's life. Parvus, too, is desperate to gain Lenin's cooperation. ('Lenin – the foundation of the whole Plan. If he recoiled, who then would carry out the revolution?'[39]) Here we have a picture of two parties desperately keen to come to an agreement, but encountering hazards which at first seem difficult to overcome. Lenin objects first of all to the idea of any collaboration with other socialists, which was part of Parvus's plan. Second, he is not convinced that Parvus is really a socialist, since Parvus believed that the revolution could and should be confined to Russia, among other heresies. Third, Lenin did not believe that Imperial Germany really wanted to overthrow the Russian monarchy: 'all it needs is peace with Russia'.[40] But most important of all, Lenin did not want to be just a pawn in Parvus's master plan – an instrument for his purposes – although Parvus tried to reassure him by saying that he himself was only concerned with German affairs.[41] However, if so, it did not prevent Lenin from further negotiation and acceptance of practical help. This behaviour by Lenin stands in marked contrast to the attitude of most European social democrats, who rightly viewed Parvus as an agent of the German General Staff. (Rosa Luxemburg, we are told, showed Parvus the door.) Parvus agrees that his own reputation is irretrievably damaged by his contacts with the Germans, but argues that his money is 'clean'.[42] In the end Lenin had refused to become personally involved, fearing the political consequences and the reproaches of his fellow socialists. But the matter had not ended there, for Parvus had asked Lenin to recommend some likely collaborators, including Hanecki. Lenin advised against Bukharin, obviously regarding him as a man of scruple.

According to Solzhenitsyn, the plot then unfolded as follows: Parvus set up an import–export agency in Copenhagen (Denmark was neutral), Hanecki became commercial director, and the firm was joined by the brothers Georg, Valdemar and Heinrich Sklarz. The office carried out a series of operations including trade with Russia and Germany, sending its agents, quite legally, through the good offices of Petrograd lawyer Koslovskii, to Russia and back.[43] The agency also allowed for an account (containing German money) to be opened at the Siberian Bank in Petrograd, which could be drawn by a lady friend of Hanecki's, Sumenson, and from her it could be transferred to important revolutionaries such as Uritskii in the Putilov works. The trouble was that Parvus lacked the right sort of contacts, so that for this reason, rather little money was paid out of the relevant account. A German foreign office official thereupon concluded, cynically, that Parvus was not really planning to create revolution in Russia, but simply to line his own pockets; so that suddenly in 1916, the cash supplies from the German Ministry of Foreign Affairs dried up. The official concerned was Secretary of State, Gottfried von Jagov.

However, this state of affairs did not last long, according to Solzhenitsyn. Parvus was doing very well on a personal level: his own financial position was improving, while his legal social-democratic newspaper *The Bell* continued to appear, taking a line which Lenin would have described as 'social-chauvinist' with respect to German war-aims. In 1916 Parvus obtained German citizenship, and he dreamed of becoming a leading figure in German social democracy. He built links with the Danish trade unions, and even founded in Copenhagen an institute for the study of the consequences of war! Most important of all, he knew that the German General Staff were not in complete agreement with the changed Foreign Office attitude to subversion in Russia, and he had a powerful ally in the German representative in Copenhagen, Count Brockdorff. In late 1916 von Jagov resigned and was replaced by Zimmerman. Solzhenitsyn does not make a great deal of the German manoeuvres, personalities and debates; for example he does not mention at this or the crucial later stage (the 'sealed' train) the roles of Ludenorff in the General Staff or Diego Bergen in the Foreign Office. The reason for this omission is fairly clear: Solzhenitsyn sees the role of Imperial Germany and of the leading German characters in the drama as essentially secondary to that of Parvus. The Germans aimed to carry out, and ultimately did carry out, the first stages of Parvus's plan. But Parvus still needed Lenin, for few socialists would have anything to do with Parvus: he was glad to receive just a few newspapers from Shlyapnikov.[44] Once again, however, Lenin refused Parvus's proposals, believing apparently that the Swiss party was more fruitful ground for the instigation of revolution than the Russian organisations. 'To begin *here* the revolution! And from here all Europe would catch alight!'[45]

In the chapters from *March 1917*, we see Lenin's motions to the Swiss Social-Democrat Party defeated, largely by the intervention of Grimm, whom Lenin then sought to exclude from the leadership of the Zimmerwald left by referendum, which would also reconvene the Swiss Social-Democrat Conference. Lenin's intricate political manoeuvres – the arguments of his 'front men', Zinoviev, Radek and Münzenburg, that any delay would be damaging to the cause of international socialism, and the lack of solidarity on this issue by the 'Skittle Club' members – are drawn in critical detail by Solzhenitsyn, who again here reveals that he sees politics as barren, dishonest and dangerous. Lenin then became involved, somewhat unsuccessfully, in agitation among Swiss militia and armed forces. However, any momentary depression that he might have felt about his lack of progress was apparently dispelled, according to Solzhenitsyn, by the suggestion from Alexandra Kollontai that the

E

Swedish Social-Democrat Party and its youth movement might provide him with more fertile ground.[46]

On 2 March 1917 (15 March, new style), the famous visit by Bronskii occurred, reporting revolution in Russia. Solzhenitsyn shows Lenin in a kind of emotional and intellectual turmoil, hungry for information, desperate to get to Russia. 'Be one week late, and you lose everything!'[47] He is dismissive of the Swiss and Switzerland, 'this republic of lackeys, whose workers are content to gather up the crumbs from the rich man's table'.[48] Such surpluses for the workers as social services, medical care, and so on, should not in Lenin's opinion be sufficient to put off the proletariat. In fact the proletariat have the right to extort even necessities from the former ruling classes. He quotes Marat with approval: 'A man has the right to wrest from others not only what is surplus, but also what is necessary. In order not to perish himself, he has the right to cut another man's throat and devour his twitching body.'[49] If indeed Lenin did approve of these sinister sentiments, this sheds prophetic light on the *de facto* application of the policy of War Communism in the Civil War period by Bolshevik gangs, when not only peasant *surpluses* were expropriated. And perhaps it also looks ahead to the sombre 1930s, when cannibalism was not unknown in the collectivisation-induced famine in the Ukraine.

Lenin regretted now that he had not travelled to Sweden six months earlier, as Parvus had proposed; he frantically opposed any idea of collaboration with the provisional government. He feared that the Tsar might not after all have abdicated, and still planned separate peace with Germany. His wild plans, for travel to Russia via France, England and Norway, or via Germany disguised as a deaf-mute Swede, are well known, but once again only in the West. He believed that the February revolution had been fomented by the British and the French, who believed perhaps that a government of Octobrists and Kadets would conduct the war with greater effect than the Tsar. Lenin the great intriguer is seen as erratic and paranoid in his judgement, suspecting plots on all sides, even on the part of the naïve and patriotic Nicholas II.

Only after the suggestion of Martov, that the journey to Russia should be effected via Germany in a sealed train, do we see Lenin beginning to pull himself together. Once again Lenin is lucky, because the negotiations were cleverly handled in Berne by his 'enemy' Grimm, and Weiss, and on 14 (27) March, when Lenin had just formulated his political programme, he received the vital visit from Sklarz. Solzhenitsyn reports this visit from Sklarz in definite terms, presumably on the basis of one of his quoted German sources. Zinoviev was present, and Sklarz's detailed proposals, together with Lenin's counter-proposals, are laid bare. (Payne has written, 'No record of Sklarz's meeting with Lenin has survived, and perhaps no record was ever made.'[50] Lenin, it seemed, was concerned not at all with the ethics of taking German money and help under the overall guidance of Parvus's plan; he was concerned only at this stage with selling the deal to the international socialist movement and otherwise concealing it as much as possible. While this is not quite tantamount to saying that Lenin was a German agent, it does show that Lenin was compliant with the then existing German war aims.

New negotiations opened, again via Grimm in Berne, for an 'extra-territorial' railway car to take up to forty passengers. By 18 (31) March, the German side was in a desperate hurry, and put a new package of proposals to Lenin over the phone through the mediation of the German socialist Paul Levi. Very soon the final solution was found through the formula of appointing Platten as travel director of the party, since Platten was a respected member of the Swiss parliament. As the world knows, the party, consisting largely of Bolsheviks and including Inessa Armand, left Switzerland on 27 March (9 April) on its tortuous journey which was to end at the Finland station seven days later. Although there were some protesters on the platform, Lenin could afford to ignore them: his course and his plans for subverting the democratic revolution were already set. Solzhenitsyn reports that Radek said to Lenin, 'In six months, either we shall be ministers, or we shall hang.'[51]

SUMMARY

Solzhenitsyn depicts Lenin in the year of the Russian revolution as a man who is fanatically dedicated to international revolution but doubtful that it could begin in Russia. He is perpetually involved in political intrigue against some of his socialist colleagues and in persuading the rest by dubious means to adopt resolutions of which he conceals the true import. He is seen as a Jacobin rather than as a Marxist, largely unconcerned with the social conditions of the countries in which he hopes to create upheaval. He is seen as a creature of moods, depressed by failures at one moment, carried away by fantastic schemes at another. He is shown as ruthless and determined, largely indifferent to human suffering, contemptuous of people with scruples, prepared to consider any means, including *de facto* collaboration with the Germans, to achieve his political aims. He is seen on occasion as a poor judge of character, lacking understanding of human beings and failing to retain any real friends. He is shown as paranoid and suspicious, suspecting others of political intrigue where none exists. He is shown, finally, as a man dedicated from the beginning to his own version of revolution, or rather a *coup d'état* against the provisional government, and the manipulation of the Soviets as a means of wielding power. He planned from the beginning to create civil war in Russia, and dreamed of extensive international subversion in a way which borders on the obsessive or even the insane. This picture of Lenin is so much at variance with any existing Soviet account that it will have a profound effect in Russia.

NOTES

1   *Bodalsya telyonok s dubom*, YMCA, Paris (1975), p. 339.
2   *Ibid.*, p. 43.
3   *Ibid.*, p. 193.
4   *Lenin v Tsyurikhe*, YMCA, Paris (1975), p. 224.
5   *Istoriya Kommunisticheskoi Partii Sovietskogo Soyuza*, Moscow, Politizdat (1970).
6   *Ibid.*, p. 193.
7   L. N. Tolstoi, *War and Peace*, Pan (1972; from translation by Constance Garnett, 1904), pp. 881–4.
8   *Lenin v Tsyurikhe, op. cit.*, p. 7.
9   *Ibid.*, p. 17.
10 *Ibid.*, p. 19.
11 A. Ulam, *Lenin and the Bolsheviks*, Fontana (1966); B. Wolfe, *Three who Made a Revolution*, Pelican (1966); R. Payne, *The Life and Death of Lenin*, Pan (1964).
12 *Lenin v Tsyurikhe, op. cit.*, p. 32.
13 *Ibid.*, p. 47.
14 *Ibid.*, p. 52.
15 *Ibid.*, p. 56.
16 *Ibid.*, p. 57.
17 *Ibid.*, p. 61.
18 *Ibid.*
19 *Ibid.*, p. 64.
20 *Ibid.*, p. 67.
21 *Ibid.*, p. 68.
22 *Ibid.*, p. 75.
23 *Ibid.*, p. 78.
24 *Ibid.*, p. 81.
25 *Ibid.*, p. 85.
26 *Ibid.*
27 *Ibid.*, p. 86.
28 *Ibid.*, p. 88.
29 *Ibid.*, p. 91.
30 *Ibid.*, p. 95.
31 *Vide*, for example, Payne, *op. cit.*, p. 274.
32 *Lenin v Tsyurikhe, op. cit.*, p. 113.
33 *Ibid.*
34 *Ibid.*, pp. 114–16.
35 *Ibid.*, p. 118.
36 *Ibid.*, p. 110.
37 *Ibid.*, p. 125.
38 *Ibid.*
39 *Ibid.*, p. 128.
40 *Ibid.*, p. 134.
41 *Ibid.*, p. 139.
42 *Ibid.*, p. 140.
43 *Ibid.*, p. 144.
44 *Ibid.*, p. 152.
45 *Ibid.*, p. 156.

46 Kollontai was referring to the proposed Congress of the Swedish Social-democrat youth party for the formation of a new party on the principles of Zimmerwald (12 May 1917).
47 *Lenin v Tsyurikhe, op. cit.,* p. 182.
48 *Ibid.,* p. 178.
49 *Ibid.,* pp. 177–8.
50 *Vide* R. Payne, *op. cit.,* p. 274.
51 *Lenin v Tsyurikhe, op. cit.,* p. 222.

13 Solzhenitsyn in Zürich and abroad

As from the summer of 1973, when a powerful attack was launched against Solzhenitsyn and Sakharov in the USSR, it seemed that the Soviet world had become too small a place to accommodate both Solzhenitsyn and the Soviet authorities. From September 1973 the struggle entered a crucial stage, which culminated in Solzhenitsyn's enforced exile to West Germany and thence to Zürich in February 1974. During this period, Solzhenitsyn's thought and action also entered a new phase, beginning with his (at first unpublished) 'Letter to Soviet Leaders' and the essay 'Peace and Violence'.

In this essay Solzhenitsyn puts forward the important idea, which lies at the root of all his subsequent comments upon détente and cold war, that the *real and logical* antithesis to peace is not necessarily 'hot war' as such, but simply violence – that is, violence of all kinds. He refers to 'systematic state violence'[1] in the USSR against its citizens. In an echo of the inter-war Litvinov doctrine, he proclaims that violence is indivisible and that any genuine coexistence between nations must mean coexistence without war and without violence. Similarly, détente must mean what it says, namely the adoption of peaceful attitudes and actions by both sides equally. People who fail to understand this are guilty, he says, of an 'emotional mistake'[2] and are deceiving themselves. In general, he says, the desire for genuine understanding and insight is overshadowed in the West by the spirit of concessions and compromise: 'an enfeebled world paints sentimental pictures of how violence will generously allow itself to be softened up and be only too happy to give up some of its superior power – which allows us in the meantime to continue with our careless existence.'[3]

Since Sakharov had continuously struggled against the internal violence of the Soviet state, and had constantly begged the West to help in this fight for human rights, Solzhenitsyn proposed that Sakharov be awarded the Nobel Peace Prize. The subsequent award of the Nobel Prize to Sakharov demonstrates the force of Solzhenitsyn's argument, and suggests that his general thesis on this point is gaining ground in the West. However, another contention of Solzhenitsyn in this speech, namely his monistic view of history and his assertion that the West must eventually follow the same path of development as the USSR, is more open to doubt. For example, he makes a direct comparison between the state of the USA today and the last years of Tsarism in Russia. This is not a parallel between social structures, but something of more fundamental importance, namely the

> psychological licence of politicians and their lack of emotional reflection. The Democrats' whole storm of anger over the Watergate affair, for example, strikes me [Solzhenitsyn] as a parody of the furious and unthinking storm the Kadets [Constitutional Democratic Party in the Imperial Duman] raised against Goremykin and Sturmer in 1915–16.[4]

(There is no implied support for Nixon in this comment.) He further criticises the USA for having reduced their politics to a struggle of interests and having inadequate regard to the fate of the nation as a whole. He refers to the USA as 'a democracy without a binding ethical base', and he condemns a situation where the struggle of interests is 'resolved only by the articles of the Constitution, with no ethical arch above it'.[5] Here there arises a fascinating and central question in the study of Solzhenitsyn's politics: does this comment show that he fails to understand both modern political science and the West? or does he understand us only too well? At first sight, the comparison between pre-revolutionary Russia and President Nixon's America seems far-fetched; and it seems that Solzhenitsyn does not know with what respect citizens of the USA cherish their constitution. All the same it is perhaps too premature to dismiss out of hand that last awkward question, and to suppose that Solzhenitsyn does not understand us at all. Solzhenitsyn's comments relate not so much to the political plane as to the moral plane: the USA must find a new ethical basis to its social and national life; protest in the USSR must be a moral and not a political protest. In answer to a question, 'How can your compatriots and youth show their support for you?', Solzhenitsyn answered,

> Definitely not by any physical acts but by rejecting the lie, and by refusing to participate personally in the lie. . . . In breaking with the lie, we are performing a moral act, not a political one and not one that can be punished by criminal law.[6]

When Solzhenitsyn was pressed on the question of the consequences of his own acts for the policy of détente and world peace, he responded, 'It is not those who talk about crimes that have been committed who harm peace and good relations between people and nations, but those who committed, or are committing, these crimes.'[7] He added that the policy of silence and concealment about the past, hitherto pursued by the USSR, did not create an atmosphere of trust and confidence.

The circumstances surrounding Solzhenitsyn's exile in February 1974 are clearly documented in the personal record *The Oak and the Calf* mentioned in the first chapter. The impression remains that the Soviet authorities were forced into a rash action by the storm of Western opinion about Solzhenitsyn's arrest. Nevertheless they evidently hoped that Solzhenitsyn's influence would decline both inside the USSR in his absence, and in the alien West. An able servant of Soviet power, Boris Korolev, wrote in the Ottawa *Citizen* (5 February 1974):

> One should talk about Aleksandr Solzhenitsyn in the past tense.... A Solzhenitsyn in the West is not a Solzhenitsyn in the USSR. How long will his decline take? A month? Three months? It depends on the efforts and means which his sponsors devote to the revitalisation of this political corpse.[8]

However, the 'political corpse' refused to remain silent in his putative grave. Instead, Solzhenitsyn's activity and vitality appeared to double and redouble. He has continued to write and to publish, to influence public opinion and perhaps government policies in many Western countries, and to carry on a dialogue with friends and compatriots. I will deal with these debates first.

Many of the Russian dissidents have attempted to find means of influencing the future of their country in ways different from Solzhenitsyn. For example, there appeared in the influential emigré Christian journal *Vestnik Russkogo Khristianskogo Dvizheniya* ('Herald of the Russian Christian Movement'),* No. 97, an attempt to analyse the ills and hopes for recovery of Russia. This series of articles, collected together by a group of Russian intellectuals, had a format similar to the famous collection of essays, *Vekhi* ('Landmarks'). Its contributors included O. Altaev, V. Gorskii, M. Chelnov, A. Ustinov, and 'N.N.' A certain pseudonymous writer Kh.U. took up this idea, suggesting that the journal could be used as a forum for new ideas and political pressures and influence as regards the future development of Russia. Thus the socially concerned intelligentsia could live without losing their self-respect and carry out their social duty, finding an answer to that perennial Russian question, 'What is to be done?'

Solzhenitsyn rebuked such notions in a subsequent number of *Vestnik* (No. 111, 1974), just as he has attacked the authors of the original collection in his essay *The Smatterers*.[9] Solzhenitsyn considered that the authors of the collection in *Vestnik* No. 97 had put forward 'a harmful and ignorant distortion of the meaning of recent Russian history'.[10] He deplored the point of view that the people of the USSR had been guilty

* Then called the 'Russian Student Christian Movement' (1970).

before the intelligentsia (an opinion expressed in the collection), and spluttered with indignation at the notion that the Orthodox Church needed to regain the confidence of the intelligentsia. In general he lashed out at the arrogance of the present-day Russian intelligentsia, who were proposing to use an Orthodox journal for their own purposes while taking no substantial risks themselves. In this connection he believes that pseudonyms should not be used, and he accused the mysterious Kh.U. of deferring to the party organs and to the leftist opinion of the West, which tends to react unfavourably to any manifestation of 'anti-Sovietism'.

Late in 1974, a response to Solzhenitsyn appeared from Pavel Litvinov, a celebrated young Russian dissident and son of the former Foreign Minister. Litvinov, who took part in the Red Square demonstration against the Soviet invasion of Czechoslovakia in 1968, and who is now living in the West, protested at the harsh tone of Solzhenitsyn and his constant demand for objective moral standards which Litvinov thought was too rigid and did not allow for human weakness. He makes a distinction between Solzhenitsyn the subtle and humane writer, and Solzhenitsyn the inflexible moralist. He objects to the phrase 'harmful and ignorant distortion of the meaning of recent Russian history'. He believes that heroic sacrifice of the type advocated by Solzhenitsyn was precisely the sort of thing that the original *Vekhi* writers were objecting to as an undesirable characteristic of the pre-revolutionary intelligentsia. He thinks that Solzhenitsyn is unfair to those who work quietly 'underground' in Russia through samizdat. (Solzhenitsyn considers that people should work openly.) Litvinov pointed out that it was those who were less well known who faced the greatest dangers and that this is why they had to keep a low profile. He points out that many of these lesser-known figures were helpful to Solzhenitsyn, for example in providing him with evidence with which to write the *Gulag Archipelago*. He criticised Solzhenitsyn for saying that those who lose heart and emigrate to the West can no longer be called 'Russians', a statement which he attributed wrongly to Solzhenitsyn, saying that this view had been expressed in a CBS interview with Walter Cronkite. Litvinov finishes with the words, 'I am sure there will come great goodness into the world, if preaching goodness is always accompanied by the habit of human kindness.'[11]

It seems to me that Kh.U. is a person close to Litvinov, and may even be Litvinov himself; but in any case there is no doubt that here is expressed the opinion of many Russian dissidents who are alarmed at Solzhenitsyn's apparent moral absolutism, his harshness and his unwillingness to suffer fools gladly. Solzhenitsyn replied at some length in February 1975, trying, it seems, to dispel some of these criticisms. However, although Litvinov's letter is fully answered, some would say that the total effect of the reply was censorious.

Oddly, Solzhenitsyn denies that he is laying down a 'system of normative ethics'. He rejected the claim that his programme ('Live not by lies') is *too* dangerous for most people: indeed it is an essential minimum, 'otherwise we sink below the level of audibility . . .'.[12] He goes further to say that the courage of those who have taken an open stand, and are alive and well, shows up the weakness and cowardice of others. He referred to the detailed criticism of *Vestnik* No. 97 in his essay *The Smatterers*, arguing that these articles did indeed present a 'harmful and ignorant distortion', and he reiterates that those who take it upon themselves to expound history should do so openly, although pseudonyms are not *always* undesirable in other forms of writing. Solzhenitsyn believes that Litvinov misread the message of the *Vekhi* writers, who after all had tended to condemn revolutionary heroism and sacrifice in favour of 'Christian conviction, self-restraint, and renunciation'.[13] This is precisely what Solzhenitsyn is advocating. He denies that he ever said that those Russians who emigrate should be denied the name 'Russian'; but he does say that his main concern is with the 250 million who remain in the Soviet Union. He denies that he has been needlessly unkind, and in a powerful and telling passage he upbraids Litvinov and demands greater things from him. 'It is shameful to waste one's diminishing years on crowds and gossip.'[14]

Solzhenitsyn also continued his fertile debate with Sakharov in 1974, and in the journal *Kontinent*, No. 2, he clarified their differences. These differences may be dealt with under four headings. First, he disagrees that Marxist ideology is powerless and irrelevant in the USSR today, a view put forward by Sakharov. 'If everyone disbelieves and everyone submits, this indicates not the weakness of Ideology but its terrifying evil power.'[15] Second, unlike Sakharov, Solzhenitsyn does not believe that full democracy is yet possible in the USSR. Without strong authority the USSR would tear itself apart, in particular because of the hostility between nationalities. (In this context, Solzhenitsyn draws approving attention to the article by M. Agurskii in *Vestnik* No. 112.) Solzhenitsyn is not opposed to democracy, but he does not think that the USSR is ready for it; and he reiterates his view that democracy is a potentially unstable form of government which can easily degenerate into totalitarianism. He suggests that authoritarianism in itself does not lead to harmful results. This unusual view is another crucial key to understanding Solzhenitsyn's politics. Third, Solzhenitsyn rejects the charge of 'White Russian nationalism'. Instead, he claims that he is simply a 'humble patriot'. Fourth, he is doubtful that one can achieve what Sakharov desires, namely a scientific and democratic regulation of the economy aided by an influx of foreign capital, and he repudiates this last aim as undesirable for Russia while strongly rejecting the charge that he is 'isolationist'.

Solzhenitsyn also attempted in the course of 1974 and 1975 to influence the policies of the Russian Orthodox Church abroad. In his 'Letter to the 3rd Congress of the Russian Church abroad'[16] in 1974, and his 'Letter from America'[17] in 1975, he placed great emphasis on the role of an Orthodox Church free from state intervention of all kinds in the Russian society of the future, claiming that it was the Petrine integration of the church into the state apparatus, and the reforms in the services undertaken by Nikon under Peter the Great, which led directly to the collapse of moral authority of the church in pre-revolutionary days. Now, he said, the situation is quite different, in the sense that public opinion about Christianity in the USSR had become quite favourable and there were many believers, possibly more proportionately than in the West. However, the Church inside Russia was still subservient to an atheist state, and he advocated as a countervailing force the unification of the three Russian churches abroad and an attempt to rediscover their Russianness and to influence the seventy million Orthodox believers, so exerting influence of a moral and spiritual kind on the future of Russia. He is convinced that 'For the world history of the twentieth century, Russia is the key country.'[18] This plausible view is also a vital key to understanding Solzhenitsyn's politics and the accent he places upon Russian national rejuvenation.

As regards the West, Solzhenitsyn has had much to say and has developed some interesting ideas on our civilisation and its origins, faults, immediate future and present policies. In a letter to *Aftenposten* he developed his ideas on détente still further, claiming that such a policy was not only ineffective but also positively dangerous, comparable to the spirit of Munich, the spirit of concessions which still lead to disaster. 'If today they crack our bones, then it is a certainty that tomorrow they will crack yours.'[19] In a speech to Italian journalists (May 1974) he pointed out that the differences between capitalism in the West and socialism in the East were important, but that we had overlooked some of the similarities. 'Both systems are defeated by a defect which is even a common defect.'[20] This defect is the materialistic world outlook and its corollaries, namely the elevation of man above all else and the sacrifice of moral principles to present indulgence, the pursuit of present interest in a selfish and wasteful way, and the accent on an ecologically harmful economic growth and industrialisation. He traces the materialism of the West and of modern man to the end of the Middle Ages, when mankind turned away from the perversion of medieval theocracy and, from the Renaissance, plunged into 'matter' and away from the world of the 'spirit'. Now men must try to regain some of their former spiritual insight. He characterises the course of events since the Middle Ages as 'Renaissance–Reformation–Enlightenment–physical bloody revolutions–democratic societies–socialist attempts'.[21] In this speech Solzhenitsyn sounds a new note, the note of apocalypse, convinced that we are on the brink of a crisis, a major transformation, a political, economic, military and spiritual upheaval, similar to the transition from the Middle Ages to the Renaissance. In order to stand firm in this crisis we all need, he says, to undergo a moral revolution.[22]

In a CBS interview with Walter Cronkite in June 1974, Solzhenitsyn pursued his theme of the imminent crisis and weakness in the West. He told Cronkite that the West had never been weaker militarily and psychologically, and that nothing substantial could therefore be expected from the Nixon visit to Russia.[23] He also criticised once again the policy of détente, pointing out that supervision and control of any agreements made by Russia with the West would be impossible. He criticised the Western press for its double standards in reporting Eastern affairs in an excessively careful and mealy-mouthed way as compared with the sensationalism of their exposés in the West. And he clarified his views on emigration. In line with his views about the necessity to pursue a tough moral policy in respect of the USSR, he attacked Zhores Medvedev in the London *Times* in September 1974 for suggesting that the award of the Nobel Peace Prize to Sakharov would be politically provocative and dangerous to the policy of détente.

The clearest statement of Solzhenitsyn's views in exile came in November 1974, when Solzhenitsyn gave a press conference in Zürich on the occasion of the publication of the collection *From Under the Rubble*. This press conference followed one in Moscow (14 November 1974), at which the other authors of the collection had spoken. As in the case of the Nobel Prize speech in 1972, this collection, clearly so important to Solzhenitsyn and his followers and co-workers such as Igor Shafarevich, caused little sensation in the West. Indeed it was barely understood. However, the press conference itself certainly clarified a number of points which I summarise as follows:

Press conference in Zürich, 16 November 1974

(1) Solzhenitsyn claims that his remarks and those of his colleagues are not political at all, but primarily moral.

(2) Hence, the terms 'left' and 'right' do not apply, they have lost their meaning.

(3) Many problems of society and the economy, such as inflation, are not primarily problems which governments or politics can solve: they are psychological or moral problems.

(4) His proposed programme of action can be summarised in his manifesto 'Live not by lies' and his essay on 'Repentance and self-limitation'.

(5) He advocates moral revolution but declares himself opposed to any form of political revolution for any reason.

(6) He hopes for nothing, no help in particular from the West. Although moral support and publicity from the West is always gratefully received, Russians will have to reform themselves.

(7) There is no hope for reform from above, as the Medvedev brothers proposed. He regards Marxist oppositions as ineffective.

(8) He regards the 'Democratic Movement', active in Russia in the 1960s and associated with the *Chronicle of Current Events*, as no longer effective, and pointed out that at least half of its active members were now abroad.

(9) Despite the power of Marxism and its influence in the USSR, if sufficient people refused to 'live by lies' – he mentions a figure in the ten thousands – 'it would change our country *in months*, not years'.[24]

(10) He condemns once again the moral relativism of the West and in particular of Amnesty International, who he says tend to equate the scale of political repression in all countries, East and West. He begs the West finally to take note of what is happening in Eastern Europe and the USSR.

In an interview with Janis Sapiets of the BBC on the day after this press conference, Solzhenitsyn summarised his views again, and made the interesting comment that Marxism is the most dangerous and the best disguised of all the totalitarian ideologies. It has proved in practice to be tyrannical, but its aims sound so reasonable and its justifications so simple and compelling. Solzhenitsyn also further clarified the meaning of his difficult concept of 'national guilt' outlined in the essay 'Repentance and self-limitation'. The example he gave was that of the British action in forcibly repatriating Russian prisoners from Austria in 1945. In the camps of the Gulag Archipelago, those repatriated said '*The British* betrayed us'. Solzhenitsyn went on to say, 'we do get the feeling that the *entire* British nation has committed a sin because it has not repented for it, has not investigated it, has not renounced it, has not tried to put it right'.[25]

In the Stockholm press conference of 12 December 1974, Solzhenitsyn clarified his views on communism, rejecting not only Stalin's legacy in the USSR but also that of Lenin *and* Marx. He denied that any Marxist regime had shown how it might be possible to create socialism 'without the wholesale robbery of the peasantry, without the enslavement of the working class, without the introduction of mass slave ownership, and without terror'.[26] He went on to say that 'anyone who reads Marx carefully will find some perfectly Leninist formulations and Leninist tactics, continuous appeals for terror, violence, and power seized by force'.[27] He thus rejects Marxism wholesale and suggests that Marxist dissidents such as R. Medvedev had set themselves a quite impossible task in respect of reforming the USSR. He went as far as to say that Medvedev himself had become merely a (flexible and intelligent) apologist for the present regime. At the same time, Solzhenitsyn strongly criticised the West for its great 'internal aridity',[28] its restlessness and dissatisfaction with life, and for the fact that in the life of the West there did not seem to be time to think about the really important questions of human existence. Solzhenitsyn thus condemns both East and West, once again prescribing his moral revolution and the abandonment of attempted solutions to social problems by physical revolutions. 'I am convinced that in order to save both the East and the West (which is also in a very dangerous situation), there is no way other than a religious and moral renaissance.'[29]

Reporters at this conference showed some impatience with Solzhenitsyn's refusal to be drawn and committed as to his political views. For example, Solzhenitsyn reiterated his belief that inflation in the West at a time of general abundance is merely a symptom of the moral and psychological failings of people in the West. However, this contention was not backed up by any substantiating argument. One questioner asked him if he considered that the Tsarist regime was better than the Soviet regime. Solzhenitsyn merely referred this person to *Gulag Archipelago*, Part III, without committing himself to any short summary of views. Finally he protested that 'Some of the questions . . . are of a far too political character – so much so that they simply have nothing to do with me.'[30]

When Solzhenitsyn appeared in Paris in April 1975, in contrast to his quieter visit to France in December 1974 and January 1975, he gave another press conference (10 April 1975) and appeared on television where he was interviewed by Jean Daniel. Raymond Aron in *Le Figaro* criticised M. Daniel for giving the interview a political slant. 'Solzhenitsyn is not a politician even if his speeches, books, life, seem to be concerned with practical politics.'[31] Aron went on to say that Solzhenitsyn's views about Vietnam, Portugal or Chile might be mistaken, but that his basic information remains: for fifty years the Western intelligentsia have refused to face up to the evidence about the Gulag Archipelago, and the question about its justification. The West's refusal to face facts, and its amazing weakness, now became for Solzhenitsyn dominant themes. He attacked the Western press for failing to publish pictures of the Ukrainian famine in the 1930s, induced artificially by collectivisation; but he attributed this blindness to a universal human trait, namely the inability of the happy and contented to understand those who are suffering. His conclusions about the West's surprising degree of weakness are, however, startling, novel and original. It is well known that Solzhenitsyn regards all forms of communism as essentially the same (he believes that China, too, has its Gulag Archipelago).[32] Thus he feels able to refer to 'the Communist system', and compares its progress to the retreat of the West since 1945.

. . . beginning in 1945, without any world war, the Western powers, under the influence of Western public opinion, have voluntarily ceded one position after another, one country after another. . . on the other hand, the Communist system has spread throughout vast territories, to the whole Far East. . . . The victorious countries [i.e. of the West] have voluntarily become defeated countries. The position of the Western victor-nations is now such as it would have been had they just lost a world war.[33]

In May 1975, Solzhenitsyn pursued this theme still further and in more detail, when a short article entitled 'A Third World War?' appeared in the *New York Times* (31 May 1975). He compared the performance of the West in resisting communist insurgency and Soviet influence in Greece (1947), West Berlin (1949), South Korea (1950), with subsequent collapse in a long list of countries. He also made predictions about imminent take-overs in Taiwan, Thailand, Malaysia, Indonesia and the Philippines. More contentiously he pointed to possible absorption (or take-over by indigenous communist parties in Europe) of Austria, Finland and Portugal. He chided the West for its apparent paralysis in the face of such threats, and its lack of unity as shown by its pathetically fissiparous response to the Arab oil embargo. He asked rhetorically whether NATO still existed, and concluded: 'It's too late to ask: how to avoid a Third World War? It is necessary to find the sobriety and courage to prevent a Fourth. To prevent it and not fall to our knees.'[34]

Solzhenitsyn's next public appearance took place in the USA in June and July 1975.* An early event of major importance in this visit was the refusal of President Ford to meet Solzhenitsyn, since the President had been advised by the National Security Council that such an action would be damaging to détente. Soon after this, Solzhenitsyn addressed a meeting of the AFL/CIO in Washington (30 June 1975). On 9 July he spoke to the New York AFL/CIO, and finally, after several attempts by the presidential staff to arrange a 'reconciliation' meeting, which Solzhenitsyn rebuffed, he spoke to a group of US senators on 15 July.

In the USA, Solzhenitsyn took a tough and uncompromising line against détente, and referred to communism everywhere as 'evil'. Beginning with the Washington address, Solzhenitsyn denied that the Soviet regime had ever been in the interest of workers. From the earliest days of the Bolshevik revolution, workers in Russia and the USSR had been denied rights, he said, and he quoted examples from Petrograd in March 1918 and the silencing of the Workers' Opposition and its representatives, such as Shlyapnikov, in 1921. He suggested that the Novocher-

* A very interesting and clear summary of this visit has appeared in *Survey* (Summer 1975) by John B. Dunlop, and the major speeches have been published by the YMCA press in Paris.

kassk strikes of 1962 show that strikes in the USSR are still seen as 'counter-revolutionary' (striking workers at Novocherkassk in 1962 were shot down: see chapter 5). For these reasons it is quite absurd, says Solzhenitsyn, to equate the aims of workers' organisations in the West with Soviet trade unions. He criticised the British TUC for its attitudes in this respect, and complimented the Federation of Labour for its policy towards the Soviet 'professionalnye soyuzy'. He reserved some considerable venom for Western capitalists who trade with the USSR, suggesting that such help is ultimately self-destructive. He asked what sort of a system is being accommodated by trading relations and détente:

> It was installed by armed uprising. It dissolved the Constituent Assembly. It capitulated to Germany – the common enemy. It introduced execution without trial. It crushed workers' strikes. It plundered the villages to such an unbelievable extent that the peasants revolted, and when this happened, it crushed the peasants in the bloodiest possible way. It shattered the Church. It reduced twenty provinces of our country to famine.[35]

All this occurred before the USSR was recognised by the USA in 1933, and well before the wartime alliance in 1941. Solzhenitsyn believes that Western democracies could and should have defeated, first totalitarianism in Germany, without relying on Russia, and then the USSR. Instead, says Solzhenitsyn, the Western democracies were so weak and so lacking in self-confidence that they strengthened Soviet totalitarianism and helped the emergence of the People's Republic of China by their inept policies. These policies, he says, have proven almost universally disastrous, and he returns here to his conclusions in the article 'A Third World War?' Solzhenitsyn stressed that the situation as he sees it is very dangerous, and that the USA will face many trials ahead, because so few nations will be able to defend themselves against communist influence. The USA should be ready for an era of struggle, and should not be diverted from her real aims and bounden duty by détente (which the USSR is using merely as a tactic in the struggle) or by such dangerous irrelevancies as the Apollo–Soyuz link-up. He cautioned against applying Western techniques and judgements to the East, as for example certain Western reporters had done when asking Russians in Moscow (in public, where they could be observed by the KGB) what they thought of the Nixon visit. Solzhenitsyn also pointed out that the US aid to Russia in the immediate post-war period ('Lend Lease') never actually reached the Soviet people!

Following up this train of thought, Solzhenitsyn refers to the Helsinki agreement as the 'funeral of Eastern Europe' – because it appeared to confirm Eastern Europe as a Soviet sphere of influence. He advocated instead a policy of firmness towards the USSR and quotes examples from Berlin to Cuba to show that, in his opinion, this attitude proved to be the safest policy. Solzhenitsyn clarifies his views about the meaning of détente in this speech, saying that it must be entirely reciprocal, including: (1) internal and external disarmament; (2) all agreements to be checked by free press, public opinion, parliaments, and so on; and (3) an end to ideological warfare. He goes on to say, '[this kind of détente] is the only way of saving the earth: to have détente instead of a world war'.[36] This comment should help to clarify Solzhenitsyn's views about détente, and to dispel criticisms that Solzhenitsyn is a warmonger. Unless genuine détente can be achieved, however, he begs us to be firm and thus take the safest possible path (it will still be dangerous) and at the same time aid the process of liberation in the USSR itself. He summarises by saying, 'Let us try to slow down the process of concessions and help the process of liberation.'[37]

The Washington speech was the subject of profuse comment and debate in the American press, and Solzhenitsyn tried to rectify some misconceptions when he addressed the New York AFL/CIO on 9 July. First, he attempted to rebut charges that he was a 'cold warrior'.

> One commentator* described me as an advocate of the cold war. This is a total misunderstanding of the world situation. The cold war is still going on, but from the other side. I can assure you the cold war has never stopped for one second in the Soviet Union.[38]

He denied most strongly that he was asking for the West to liberate the people of Russia. 'I have always told my countrymen that they must save themselves.'[39] However, he did ask for a slowing down of commercial dealings with the USSR. In a characteristically sweeping statement he said, 'Our whole slave system depends on your economic assistance.... Stop sending goods, . . . Let them stand on their own feet, and see what happens.'[40]

In the US Senate on 15 July, Solzhenitsyn stated that although he had felt highly honoured personally by the invitation and the (previous) offer of honorary citizenship, he was speaking not for himself but for the 'masses deprived of rights in my country and even in other communist countries'.[41] At the height of his fame and renown on this visit to the USA, he seemed humble, self-effacing, aware of crushing responsibility and duty. He claimed that the West could and should help people oppressed in Eastern countries who quite understood the monstrousness of the system under which they were living. He begged the senators and the American public to open their eyes to conditions in the East, and he made a plea for mutual understanding, a point which should tend to

---

* It was Joseph Kraft of the *Washington Post*, 3 July 1975.

F

answer charges that Solzhenitsyn is an isolationist and a narrow nationalist. He stressed once again that détente as presently practised by the USA meant the strengthening of the Soviet prison system and the hold of the Soviet Union over Eastern Europe. Solzhenitsyn used some graphic and startling language to portray Soviet prison conditions, but he seemed also to despair of conveying his message to a prosperous US public. 'But I did what I had to and what I could.'[42] Solzhenitsyn's by now characteristic note of warning and apocalypse crept in during the final part of this speech: he predicted great problems ahead for the USA which would dwarf the Vietnam experience; and this would occur because, like it or not, the USA is the leader of the free world. He talked of the 'coming combination of world political crisis and spiritual revolution of mankind . . .'; and he went on to warn the US senators, 'Very soon, too soon, your state needs not only unusual but great people. Search for them in your souls. Search for them in your hearts. Search for them in the depths of your fatherland.'[43]

Solzhenitsyn's activity in the West since his exile has been amazing. Apparently he works up to sixteen hours a day with the help of his wife Natalya Svetlova, and he does not receive callers. Solzhenitsyn seems to have a sense of urgency, as indicated by the fact that he has twice 'scaled down' his ambitious plans for writing a history of the course of revolution and its immediate origins from August 1914. Although he modified his originally proposed twenty 'knots', aiming to write three or four knots up to April 1917, he subsequently published with preliminary haste the chapters from the first three knots relating to Lenin, under the title of *Lenin in Zürich*. While working on his histories, his knots for 1917, he has also published in the West his personal record, *The Oak and the Calf (Bodalsya telyonok s dubom)*; the collection *From Under the Rubble*, which he edited, containing three of his essays; and the *Gulag Archipelago*, Parts II and III. Although many of these works were completed in the USSR before his exile, this effort of publication represents a monumental achievement of planned presentation and, apparently, some kind of race against time.

In September 1975, he addressed some remarks to a conference of 'Peoples enslaved by communism' held at Strasbourg (27 September). In this note he made an additional point about the weakness of the Western world, namely that its *intellectual* leadership had been lost in world affairs, while the 'habitual arrogance' of Westerners had blinded their eyes to this fact. He expressed the hope that Eastern Europe might become more united in its opposition to communism, and he asked delegates not to be lulled into complacency by the enervating atmosphere of the West.[44]

In 1976, in addition to his literary output, Solzhenitsyn's astonishing influence on public opinion continued. On 1 March 1976 he appeared on BBC-1's 'Panorama' with Michael Charlton. The interview was received with considerable attention and was widely discussed in Britain. This was followed by a Radio 3 broadcast on 25 March. Both broadcasts were repeated (8 and 1 April respectively). *The Listener*, which published some edited* versions of the talks, had to be printed in extra large numbers to meet the demand.

In the 'Panorama' interview, Solzhenitsyn reiterated that his urgent warnings go unheeded. He said that the West seemed to be going through some processes of the kind which led to revolution in 1917 in Russia. He rejected the charge that he is advocating a patriarchal form of society dominated by Russian Orthodoxy: but he also pointed out that the question of Russia's future was almost irrelevant compared with the burning question of the future of the West. In comparison with the West, Solzhenitsyn now believes that the political system of the Soviet Union looks stable and secure. What is now ruining the West above all, in Solzhenitsyn's opinion, is its pragmatic philosophy. He demanded the return of moral considerations to politics, and cited the stand against Hitler taken by Britain in 1939 as an example. Solzhenitsyn condemned Britain's habit of affording diplomatic recognition to any government which happened to be in power.

Solzhenitsyn uncharacteristically evaded a question which posed a comparison between Lenin and himself (as a kind of anti-Lenin). He replied that whereas Lenin was surprised at the news of revolution in Russia in March 1917, he had some cause to expect it. Solzhenitsyn however had no cause to expect any sudden change in the USSR, 'but I wouldn't be surprised at something else: I wouldn't be surprised at the sudden and imminent fall of the West.'[45] He urged the West to take steps to strengthen itself, and he criticised the Helsinki agreement because, among other things, it meant that Western reporters were failing to report news of persecution or to accept information from dissidents, in exchange for greater freedom of movement. He gave some frightening examples of such persecution, and of illegal actions by the KGB. He strongly attacked the slogan, attributed to Bertrand Russell, 'better red than dead', and suggested that it contained the essence of the West's surrender-mentality.

Response to this interview was swift and immediate. Many people referred to Solzhenitsyn's prophetic tone, and feared that his message would lead to an arms race or even to 'hot' war. Others proclaimed that Solzhenitsyn had failed to understand the West. Perhaps the most articulate representative of this school of thought was Professor R. A. Peace of Hull University, who placed Solzhenitsyn very firmly in the tradition of the nineteenth-century Slavophiles or Populists, such as Dostoevskii and Mikhailovskii, whose disillusionment with the West had been a

* Should such exceptional broadcasts be edited at all?

function of matching reality against their original idealised preconceptions. Professor Peace concluded, 'The way ahead lies not in physical containment but in critical comprehension [i.e. of the USSR] and for this we have adequate resources to hand if they are put to proper use.'[46] One of the clearest statements supporting Solzhenitsyn came from Professor G. H. N. Seton-Watson, who underlined again the military might of the USSR, and pointed out that even if it could be said that Solzhenitsyn misunderstood some aspect of the West, nevertheless this comment of an 'outsider' might be accurate and helpful. He concluded, 'One does not have to believe that "The West" has a monopoly of virtue, or that "communists" are wicked, in order to recognise that Soviet imperialism, many of whose servants are admirable persons, is a deadly and growing menace to us all.'[47] Other notable contributions to the debate came from Lord Gladwyn, who denied that the West need necessarily despair of defending itself; and from Bernard Levin, who pointed out that Solzhenitsyn's greatest impact had been not upon the 'pundits' but upon ordinary people, who had sensed in great numbers that Solzhenitsyn was saying something important and truthful.[48]

When Solzhenitsyn subsequently appeared on French television (19 March 1976), the USSR made a strong protest to the French government, indicating that he is thought to be having considerable influence. Solzhenitsyn has also asked the Spanish authorities to stand firm against riots and not to reform too quickly, since the danger of totalitarianism is greatest in unstable democracies. Solzhenitsyn has further alienated left-wing opinion by supporting the record of Franco's Spain and its Christian heritage. (Solzhenitsyn has always maintained that conditions in countries such as Spain, South Africa or even Chile are not comparable with the degree of totalitarian control in the USSR. This obvious fact has for some reason been denied by sections of opinion in the West. However, advice to a national government as to how best to avoid revolution does not in itself imply wholehearted support for that government.)

R. Medvedev, the Soviet Marxist–Leninist dissident, strongly attacked Solzhenitsyn's views on détente and his apparent support for right-wing authoritarian regimes (*Sunday Times*, 28 March 1976). He was answered by *The Times* correspondent Vaclav Sikl, a member of the Free Czechoslovak Air Force Association. 'As to Roy Medvedev's majority assertion "today, there is no other alternative but the road to peaceful cooperation", may I suggest that any road which all the occupation forces will take out of my country would be an excellent one to start with?'[49]

Although Mr Sikl supported the 'permanence of British commonsense, her capacities to produce, her dedication to the defence of freedom of mind', Solzhenitsyn's next broadcast (24 March 1976) attacked Britain even more strongly. Despite a kind and thankful word to the BBC Russian broadcasts, he nevertheless asked why 'societies with access to every kind of information suddenly plunge into lethargy, into a kind of mass blindness, a kind of voluntary self-deception'.[50] He reiterated here his belief that only *art* can provide some clue to this and other riddles of human nature. He remarked on the rapidity with which the West appears to have lost its strength, self-confidence and world influence. He attributed this to the materialism and atheistic humanism of the modern era, which he said had now reached its logical conclusion in both East and West. With a compelling clarity, he enumerates the process as: the era of industrialisation, colonial expansion, superficial Christianity, World War I and the Bolshevik revolution. He apparently believes that this process is monistic, thus giving an implicit credence to the possibility of prophecy. He certainly believes that some of Dostoevskii's writings were prophetic: in this respect, however, he seemed a little hurried and contentious, for he added Professor Kurganov's figures of 66 million dead in Soviet camps to 44 million war casualties in order to produce an apparent fulfilment of Dostoevskii's prophecy that 'socialism' would result in about 100 million dead. Can one thus attribute Hitler's war to socialism in Russia? It seems far-fetched to suppose that one can (for example) blame Stalin entirely for the rise of Hitler in Germany.

Solzhenitsyn's monistic view of history may possibly reflect his Marxist background, and his prophecies of imminent doom for the West neatly fit Soviet official views; but at the same time, do we not feel a disturbing note of truth in the comments which Solzhenitsyn makes about the characteristics he observes in our society?

> Adults deferring to the opinions of their children; the younger generation carried away by shallow worthless ideas; professors scared of being thought unfashionable; journalists refusing to take responsibility for the words they squander so profusely; universal sympathy for revolutionary extremists; people with serious objections unwilling or unable to voice them; the majority passively obsessed by a feeling of doom; feeble governments; societies whose defensive reactions have become paralysed; spiritual confusion leading to political upheaval.[51]

Solzhenitsyn criticised not only British society but also the actions of British governments. He attacked their adherence to pragmatism in politics and international relations, including Britain's failure, as he sees it, to support former allies (White Russians) in 1919, and the betrayal of one and a half million Russian refugees in Austria who were forcibly repatriated in 1945. He makes the comment which is of fundamental importance to an understanding of his politics: 'A moral stance, even in politics, always safeguards our spirit; sometimes, as we can see, it even protects our very existence.'[52]

Solzhenitsyn is cynical about Britain's post-war record on almost every count. Sometimes he seems less than well informed, criticising for example British quarrels with Iceland and Spain. He castigated the selective reporting of events (from the 'free press'). Then he returned to his previous themes, about Britain's *de facto* loss of the 'Third World War' and about the 'sins of the fathers being visited upon the children'. Finally he was critical of the power exerted in Britain and the West by *socialist* ideas. He himself relates 'socialism' very closely to Marxian socialism and, like Igor Shafarevich, regards socialism as a static, ancient and enslaving form of social organisation. Its originators included, he said, Thomas More, Campanella, Winstanley, Morelli, Deschamps, Baboeuf and Fourier as well as Marx. He denied that any Marxian socialism could ever be democratic, thus implicitly rejecting Roy Medvedev's recent massive exposition *On Socialist Democracy*.[53] The British respect for socialism, he said, means that they are bemused and fail to see the danger of being 'taken over' by such a system. In a passage which sounds uncomfortably like an Old Testament prophet, he said 'all of us are standing on the brink of a great historical cataclysm, a flood which swallows up civilisations and changes whole epochs'.[54]

He is perhaps unfair to Britain in belittling her to the extent of saying that she is of less significance than Uganda or Roumania, but nearer the truth when he said that 'Contemporary society in Britain is living on self-deception and illusions both in the world of politics and in the world of ideas.'[55]

SUMMARY

Solzhenitsyn in Zürich, like Lenin before him, has been a man totally dedicated to revolution; but whereas Lenin was concerned with a political revolution, Solzhenitsyn hopes to achieve a moral revolution. He believes that all governments must be based upon an ethical idea, and that democracies tend to lack this, so that they often degenerate into unedifying struggles between rival interests. He believes that authoritarian governments are preferable to unstable democracies, because it is the latter which give rise to totalitarianism. He gives no evidence for this important assertion, apparently deriving most of his conclusions from Russian experience. Because Solzhenitsyn regards all communism as evil, he feels that it should be resisted wherever possible, and on these grounds he opposes the policy of détente as practised at present by the West and points to the declining influence of the West in world affairs and her inadequate defences. His aim, however, is not to foment war but to minimise its possibility and at the same time check the spread of communism. Solzhenitsyn has clarified his differences with other

Russian dissidents such as Pavel Litvinov, Andrei Sakharov and Roy Medvedev, but he seems to be something of a distant, lonely figure to his fellow countrymen, although admired greatly by them. In this respect the comparison with Lenin remains an intriguing one.

Solzhenitsyn has developed a particularly urgent, prophetic and doom-laden tone, predicting possible imminent collapse of the West and a spiritual crisis in the affairs of men. He believes that mankind has been following a fatally incorrect path of development from the Renaissance, and that it is wrong to suppose that socialism, by which he means Marxian socialism, will provide a solution. He prescribes moral revolution as the only true solution for mankind, rejecting all kinds of other proposed solutions; and in this certainty and dedication, once again he resembles Lenin. In his disappointment with the West, he has pointed out our lack of intellectual influence and self-confidence, and he has chided us for our selfishness, short-sightedness and the tendency to embrace the 'spirit of Munich'. He has reserved particular venom for the USA (which he compares with Russia in the last years of Nicholas II) and Britain, whose consistent pragmatism in politics and international relations is anathema to him. Solzhenitsyn's views on political science seem unusual, if not wide of the mark; but his overall message, for all its messianism and sweeping generalisations, has become both clear and seemingly relevant to many ordinary citizens throughout the Western world.

NOTES

1 *Index*, No. 4 (1973).
2 L. Labedz (ed.), *Solzhenitsyn – A Documentary Record*, Penguin (1974), p. 350.
3 *Index*, No. 4 (1973).
4 *Ibid.*
5 *Ibid.*
6 *The Times* (22 January 1974).
7 *Solzhenitsyn – A Documentary Record, op. cit.*, p. 371.
8 *Citizen* (Ottawa) (5 February 1974), quoted in *ibid.*, pp. 385–7.
9 *From Under the Rubble*, Collins/Harvill (1975), pp. 229–78.
10 *Vestnik Russkogo Khristianskogo Dvizheniya*, No. 111 (1974), p. 7.
11 *Vestnik . . .*, No. 114 (1975), p. 260.
12 *Ibid.*, p. 261.
13 *Ibid.*
14 *Ibid.*, p. 264.
15 *Kontinent*, No. 2 (1974), pp. 352–3.
16 *Vestnik . . .*, No. 112, pp. 99–111.
17 *Vestnik . . .*, No. 116, pp. 121–31.
18 *Ibid.*, p. 128.
19 Letter to *Aftenposten* (25 May 1974), quoted in *Possev* (July 1974), p. 11.
20 *Vestnik . . .*, No. 111, p. 67.
21 *Ibid.*
22 *Ibid.*, p. 69.
23 *Possev* (August 1974), p. 11.

24   *Dve Press-Konferentsii*, YMCA, Paris (1975), p. 81.
25   Caris Report, BBC East European Service, 16/74, p. 7.
26   *Radio Liberty Research Supplement* (3 June 1975), p. 10.
27   *Ibid.*, p. 11.
28   *Ibid.*, p. 21.
29   *Ibid.*, p. 24.
30   *Ibid.*, p. 25.
31   *Vestnik . . .*, No. 115, p. 262.
32   *Russkaya Mysl* (17 April 1975), p. 2.
33   *Ibid.*
34   *Vestnik . . .*, No. 115, p. 257.
35   *Survey* (Summer 1975), p. 117.
36   *Ibid.*, p. 127.
37   *Ibid.*, p. 132.
38   *New York Times* (10 July 1975), p. 31.
39   *Ibid.*
40   *Ibid.*
41   *Novoe Russkoe Slovo* (19 July 1975), p.1
42   *Ibid.*
43   *Ibid.*
44   *Vestnik . . .*, No. 116, p. 252.
45   *The Listener* (4 March 1976), p. 261.
46   *The Times* (5 March 1976).
47   *The Times* (10 March 1976).
48   *The Times* (19 March 1976).
49   Letter to *The Times*, dated 29 March 1976.
50   *The Times* (2 April 1976), p. 9. (N.B. *The Listener* edited out several paragraphs of
       the interview.)
51   *Ibid.*
52   *Ibid.*
53   R. Medvedev, *On Socialist Democracy*, Macmillan (1975).
54   *The Times* (2 April 1976), p. 9.
55   *Ibid.*

14 Solzhenitsyn's intellectual tradition

No writer, thinker or artist operates in an intellectual vacuum. Everyone is subject to influences, or has affinities with predecessors and contemporaries; in this sense, no thinker is entirely and exclusively original. However, the thought of Solzhenitsyn seems to have many original, if not paradoxical, qualities, especially to those schooled in the Western tradition of political thought. Therefore it is especially helpful to place Solzhenitsyn in his own historical and national context. I have already remarked on the influence or affinity which Solzhenitsyn derives from D. N. Shipov, N. A. Berdyayev and F. M. Dostoevskii; but the Russian tradition which seems to me to be closest to Solzhenitsyn is that of the so-called 'Native Soil Movement' (*Pochvennichestvo*) which was influential in Russia in the late 1850s and 1860s, and of which F. M. Dostoevskii was a prominent representative.

In order to understand the term *Pochvennichestvo*, it is necessary to look at its origins and its development, because it is an eclectic creed which was subject to change over time. The most useful single source in understanding the nature of *Pochvennichestvo* is in an unpublished PhD thesis by Dr Wayne Dowler (London University, 1973). Dr Dowler regards the *Pochvennichestvo* as

> an extension of the general, European, romantic movement [which], like it, [expressed] the uniqueness of individuals and nations, the need for immediacy and spontaneity in intellectual and social life, the wholeness of spiritual existence and the primacy of living experience over rational analysis.[1]

Dr Dowler considers that the *Pochvennichestvo* was primarily a national–psychological doctrine, not a religious one. However, representatives of the movement had a tendency to regard the Orthodox Church as one of the essential ingredients of Russian nationality, although making a distinction between the official, established church (which in the nineteenth century was integrated into the state apparatus) and the 'humble' instinctive religiousness of the people. The founders of the movement were probably the editors of the journal *Moskvitianin* ('The Muscovite'), some time around 1850, in particular A. A. Grigor'ev and E. N. Edel'son. They were greatly concerned with the nature and origins of Russia and with the interpretation of her history, in particular the significance of the Petrine reforms which had been so bitterly attacked by the Slavophiles in the 1840s.[2]

While possessing some of the characteristics of conservative nationalists, the *pochvenniki* were also, paradoxically enough, radicals. They were opposed to the institution of serfdom, and to the bureaucratic features of the autocracy. Thus they did not equate the nation with the state as such, or with any particular form of state organisation. They believed that the essence of the nation, its native soil, was best understood and represented by the people (*narod*), and that national development could best take place on the basis of the peasant commune (*obshchina*). Thus nationalism and democratic feelings reinforced one another in this school of thought.[3] However, this is not to say that they equated the nation with its people: they said merely that the people were most likely to understand their nation best, whereas the upper classes and the intelligentsia were unable to interpret correctly the true interests of Russia.

This view of nationalism was essentially romantic rather than realistic. (How many of the young editors of *Moskvitianin* had actually worked and lived for an appreciable length of time in a peasant commune?) Their romantic nationalism derived much from the doctrines of Herder, who believed that each nation represented one of the many sides of humanity and that each had a particular contribution to make to human civilisation. Thus Herder believed that although there is a mysterious unity[4] called 'humanity', it could only be (dimly) apprehended by way of its many different manifestations, the nations of the world. The *pochvenniki* saw this as a concrete, manageable approach as opposed to the unrealistic airy abstractions which were advocated so glibly by the cosmopolitanism of the eighteenth-century enlightenment. They opposed Western rationalism and socialism, and they were particularly opposed to the Russian nihilists of their own time. In general, they hated abstractions of all kinds; they rejected ideology, believing that life was much too rich and diverse to be explained in terms of any *a priori* ideal. They therefore opposed any conclusions about society based on the class-analysis.

How did the *pochvenniki* understand the term 'nation'? Firstly they believed that the nation is a unique, united entity whose essence is unchanging over time. In this they were profoundly at variance with Hegel. What then is this mysterious 'essence', and how can it be described and expressed? The *pochvenniki* believed that the essence of a nation is revealed in national art, particularly in literature and (in Russia) the folk song. A. A. Grigor'ev was particularly adept in this latter field. The *pochvenniki* viewed art as superior to social or political programmes, believing that all sections of society have a primary need for moral, intellectual and aesthetic enlightenment.

Already, then, the outlines of the philosophy of the *pochvenniki* are apparent, and these were further developed after the demise of *Moskvitianin* in 1856 by two journals, *Vremia* ('Times') and *Epokha* ('The Era'), 1855–60.

A. A. Grigor'ev was deeply attached to the national customs of the people: he believed that any attack on these traditional practices constituted an attack on the nation as a whole. In the same way that custom is often apparently irrational, inefficient or even ritualistic, so also the essence of life is mysterious, inexplicable. It could not be adequately defined by social philosophy, science or political programmes; only art, and in particular literature, could explain and elucidate. One consequence of this belief was that the *pochvenniki* saw the artist or writer as the voice of the whole people, and in this sense art was democratic and imposed grave responsibilities on the writer. The *pochvenniki* made even grander claims for the writer: not only could literature explain contemporary national life in a way that theory could not, but also it could elucidate universal truths. For example, the *pochvenniki* greatly admired Pushkin, whom they saw as an aspect and proof of Russian universality. They believed, too, that literature could be prophetic.

Hence the *pochvenniki* rejected emphatically any notions that art could be justified only with reference to itself, the 'art for art's sake' school. Also they rejected equally emphatically the utilitarian, socially conscious art of Chernyshevskii and Dobrolyubov, believing that art and literature can never be subordinated to any social or political goals. It is linked to life, and yet autonomous. The *pochvenniki* believed, finally, that art and literature are creative of beauty which is itself inherently truthful and absolute.

The *pochvenniki* worshipped life as experienced by individuals in all their complexity, individuality and richness. They rejected Hegelianism which tended to reduce nationality and individualism, indeed the process of history itself, to the abstract workings of general laws. I believe that the *pochvenniki* would have rejected equally firmly the historical materialism of Marx, Engels and Lenin. However, while they placed great emphasis on the unique and undetermined voluntarism of individuals and nations in their social life, they believed that such actions could and should be *reasonable*. They opposed abstract theorising and rationalism, for which the Russian word is *rassudochnost'*, but they believed that reason, *rasumnost'*, should rule in human affairs.

F. M. Dostoevskii was a representative member of the *pochvenniki*. In the 1840s he had espoused the cause of cosmopolitan socialism, but at some stage in his Siberian exile he was converted to Christianity. He believed that the ideal of universal humanity was impossible without

Christianity, and attempted to apply the ideals of universal humanity to his own country, to the native soil. He considered that a great dehumanising factor in Russia was its social division, and that this must be healed. As he himself said, 'Union [of the whole people is vital] at all costs and as quickly as possible – that is our motivating idea, that is our motto.'[5] One vital factor needed to achieve this union was universal literacy and education. The *pochvenniki* rejected notions of the class struggle, and they preached the organic unity and particularity of the Russian nation. They were especially concerned with Russia, but they would have argued that their general outlook applied to any nation. All nations, they said, must understand first their own unique characteristics, and build on these in order to progress and to contribute fully to the progress of humanity as a whole. Dostoevskii believed that one of the fundamentally *Russian* characteristics was a sense of fraternity and brotherhood, so that peaceful cooperation among the various strata of Russian society might become possible.

With regard to the West, Dostoevskii believed that Russia had learned effectively all that there was to be learned from Europe and must now set about discovering and building upon its own special characteristics. In a sense the *pochvenniki* were neither Slavophiles nor Westerners. They criticised P. Ya. Chaadayev, for example, becaue he had said that, in comparison with the West, Russian life was an empty desert. What he should have said, they argued, was that Russian life was totally different from Western life, but no less human.[6] However, the *pochvenniki* thought that the Slavophiles had also been somewhat in error by reacting too strongly to Chaadayev, being subject to illusions and wishful thinking about the Russian past. Grigor'ev in particular stressed that it was impossible to put the clock back.[7] Any basis for genuine and lasting reform must be found in the real historical characteristics of the nation, which need to be studied accurately and without illusion. Whether or not the *pochvenniki* succeeded in doing this remains in doubt: they surely had many affinities with Slavophilism. Especially they believed that a rejuvenated Russia had something positive to offer to an exhausted, decadent Europe. However, we can say that although the *pochvenniki* were nationalist and conservative, at the same time they were critical of their own state and by no means reactionary.

In the West we have become accustomed to the idea that if a school of thought or body of opinion is systematically critical of an existing political regime, then such a school of thought has the characteristics of a *political movement*. However, in Russian political thought as opposed to the Western tradition, a common idea, found particularly in nineteenth-century Slavophilism, is that one can separate social from political thought – that is, one can advocate radical social change without altering political authority in any way. The *pochvenniki* belonged to this tradition. However, they insisted that any change must take place within the framework of national culture. Hence the *pochvenniki* approved of the Emancipation of 1861, seeing it as the beginning of a new national unification among social classes. But they opposed any doctrines of revolution and terrorism as advocated by the nihilists, and they conducted an energetic campaign against this school of thought. Sometimes the *pochvenniki* were referred to as 'gradualists'.[8]

The role of education and literacy in achieving national renaissance has already been stressed. This was a task for society as opposed to government: it was thought necessary by the *pochvenniki* that each individual should develop his or her own powers, and that a body of 'public opinion' should subsequently emerge as a result of this process. (They believed that special educational techniques, with a rather Tolstoyan flavour, would be required for the peasantry.) In common with Slavophilism, the *pochvenniki* believed that society was responsible for its own administration in many matters, and for its own moral self-improvement. Once again, then, we get an apparently paradoxical mixture: emphasis on social activism, public opinion, decentralisation and individual initiative; but at the same time a belief that all this can take place and leave political authority substantially unscathed. Dr Dowler puts it this way:

> The state remained for them a constant, the symbol of external order and unity, whereas the nation in their view continued to grow organically in the form of an autonomous and increasingly more perfect moral and social order. The *pochvenniki*, therefore, set politics aside and turned to the ethical reordering of society.[9]

Thus it is very difficult to pin an accurate 'label' on to the *pochvenniki* which makes sense in terms of Western political thought or science. Perhaps the nearest one can get is 'liberal conservative'. Dr Dowler attributes the following illustrative comment (from an unpublished letter) to F. M. Dostoevskii:

> The state needs the kind of conservatism which is based on national traditions, which defends everything reasonable in the past – the spirit of the people and its interests – which would examine and criticise every new demand in social life. This conservatism would be a truly conserving force.[10]

The *pochvenniki* were liberal only in that they demanded social activism, universal education, decentralisation and certain freedoms. They rejected Western liberalism with its social-contract theory and its accent on written constitutions and parliamentarianism. Such views were supported in Russia by, for example, B. N. Chicherin and K. D. Kavelin.

As far as the *pochvenniki* were concerned, such ideas were foreign importations, alien to the Russian tradition.

In economic philosophy, the *pochvenniki* were again apparently paradoxical in that they rejected both capitalism and socialism. Like many nineteenth-century Russian conservatives they were anti-capitalist, not only because of the suffering capitalism seemed to cause, but also on aesthetic grounds in that it distorted moral values, creating greedy materialism and conformism. Equally, however, they rejected socialism as mechanistic, anti-national and destructive of freedom, although they admitted that certain Western socialists had analysed accurately the malaise of capitalism. They were attracted, therefore, to some 'third' path of economic development, in particular to the ideas of P. J. Proudhon and the ideal of achieving economic growth through the peasant commune and the industrial (small-scale) artel. In other words they believed in cooperative or syndicalist enterprise, which would be made possible, so they believed (utopianism?), through the mediation of Russian good-neighbourliness and fraternity.

Thus the *Pochvennichestvo* was essentially not a political movement at all, but a social, moral and aesthetic one. As such, it was eclectic, utopian and politically ineffective, especially after the general disillusionment which followed the Great Reforms. Indeed one could argue that the *pochvenniki* subsequently retreated into a kind of messianism and mysticism, which is illustrated by a comment in a letter from F. M. Dostoevskii to N. N. Strakhov in 1869. In this letter Dostoevskii claimed that the whole of Russia's mission towards humanity was simply to reveal Christ to the world. 'In my opinion, this is the entire essence of our future role as civiliser and resurrector, so to speak, of all Europe, the entire essence of our future life.'[11] In its later development, then, the *Pochvennichestvo* became more dogmatic, and more prone to sweeping metaphysical or religious panaceas.

One can immediately see the connection between the *Pochvennichestvo* and the ideas of Solzhenitsyn, and there can be no doubt at all that he is strongly influenced by this intriguing and original body of thought. It should be noted that the earlier phase of *Pochvennichestvo* advocated a liberal nationalism, while a later phase developed a messianic and metaphysical character.

Another influential thinker was N. A. Berdyayev, whose thought also exhibited both liberal gradualism and a later messianism. When Berdyayev contributed the first essay to the *Vekhi* collection of 1909, his work had much in common with the other essays. The *Vekhi* collection has experienced a resurgence in Russia in recent years. Like the *Vekhi* writers and Berdyayev, the Russian intelligentsia today knows that it faces a conservative (party) autocracy which has very little scope for reform; it knows that radical reform would be in fact extremely dangerous. Like the *Vekhi* writers, today's would-be reformers see the scope of political action as limited, stressing the superiority of moral considerations to politics and hoping for some liberation, not only from the regime, but also from the 'oppressive power of politics' (Berdyayev[12]). Western-style politics, typified by the aims of liberal democracy and espoused by the 'Democratic Movement' and Andrei Sakharov, sometimes seems superficial and artificial in Russian conditions, much as the policies of the Kadet Party and its accent on Western-style parliamentarianism and a 'responsible ministry' seemed irrelevant and powerless in the period up to 1917.

But although Berdyayev's sentiments echo his colleagues in the *Vekhi* collection, the very title of his essay, 'Philosophical truth [*istina*] and intelligentsia truth [*pravda*]',[13] indicate his fundamentalism, for he is saying that the aim of the intelligentsia in discovering some political platform from which to fight the autocracy cannot be truthful. His whole essay in effect renounces politics and the political struggle, in favour of discovering some more fundamental and important truth. Berdyayev was not devoid of political ideas: he advocated a kind of syndicalist democracy based on locality and profession, which would allow participatory democracy and cooperative enterprise. Such a scheme would tend, Berdyayev hoped, to eliminate the class struggle, 'since both the employers and workers realise that their interests are basically identical'. The function of government would be to act as an umpire of final authority between the various factions and associations.[14] All these proposals are designed in fact for a specific end: Berdyayev believed that both capitalism and socialism were destructive of the environment and detrimental to human relationships and values, and he advocated instead a form of social and economic life which would be conducive to what he called 'integral Christianity', that is, a Christianity which is not just confined to rite and sentiment but influences deeds and life. Thus, in the end, Berdyayev is a fundamentalist, and in his influential work on the philosophical basis of the Russian revolution, first published in 1931, he summarised his conclusions as follows:

> Integral Christianity can accept all that is true in Communism and reject all that is false. If there is not a Christian revival in the world, a rebirth not only among the elite but also among the great masses of the people, atheistic Communism will conquer over the whole earth.[15]

NOTES

1 Wayne Dowler, 'The native soil movement (*Pochvennichestvo*)', PhD thesis, London University (1973), p. 12.
2 In particular I. V. Kireevskii, A. S. Khomiakov, K. S. Aksakov.

3   Richard Pipes, 'Russian Conservatism in the second half of the 19th century', *Slavic Review*, Vol. 30 (March 1971), p. 124.
4   Rheinhold Aris, *The History of Political Thought in Germany*, Cass, London (1965), pp. 241–3.
5   Dowler, *op. cit.*, p. 120.
6   *Ibid.*, p. 147.
7   *Ibid.*, p. 157.
8   P. V. Bykov, *Siluety dalekogo proshlogo*, Moscow, Leningrad (1930), p. 51.
9   Dowler, *op. cit.*, p. 196.
10 *Ibid.*, p. 198
11 Letter to N. N. Strakhov, dated 18 March 1869, quoted in *ibid.*
12 *Vekhi*, Possev, Frankfurt (1967), p. 22.
13 *Ibid.*, p. 1.
14 Matthew Spinka, *Nicholas Berdyayev, Captive of Freedom*, The Westminster Press (1950), pp. 168–9.
15 N. A. Berdyayev, *The Russian Revolution*, University of Michigan Press, Ann Arbor (1961), p. 91.

Conclusion

To explain Solzhenitsyn's intellectual tradition is not to 'explain him away'. He is one of the most important of the Russian dissidents, all of whom work in conditions of great difficulty. The moral and intellectual failure of Soviet Marxism has created a profound dilemma: should the way forward be one of cautious evolution, as Roy Medvedev believes, or is it now necessary to admit past errors and moral enormities, and achieve radical change? The tradition of revolution looks impossible to humane people, and it may be said that Lenin's example has created an intellectual vacuum. Would Western democratic forms be applicable in Russian conditions? Russia's limited experience in this respect in 1917 was disastrous, and today the Western democracies themselves seem less than stable, less than self-confident.

It is inevitable that people like Solzhenitsyn should go back to pre-revolutionary traditions, for the record of Soviet political thought since at least 1924 has been dismal and sterile. It is significant that the only alternative contemporary ideology in Russia is Christianity. In these conditions it is easy to see why the rejection of Soviet Marxism leads to a rejection of all Marxism, why the apparent failure of 'normal' political activity in pre-revolutionary Russia and in the USSR today leads to a rejection of all politics.

Yet Solzhenitsyn has still imbibed a considerable diet of Marxism. He may have been influenced by one of the messages of Marxism in that he sees the process of history as monistic, although in contradistinction to Marxists he believes this process can be altered in the remote event of a moral revolution. Where is this process leading? Like Marxists, Solzhenitsyn says that it is leading to communism unless the Western world takes urgent action. Since Solzhenitsyn's own experiences, and the last sixty years in Russia and the USSR, prove to Solzhenitsyn that communism is intolerable, he rejects quite logically the processes which preceded communism. It is this rejection of renaissance, reformation, enlightenment, the industrial revolution, which we in the West find so startling.

Solzhenitsyn's shortcomings are those of the *Pochvennichestvo*. Is it really possible to advocate radical social changes and leave the political system intact? There seems to be considerable lack of thought in the

political arena: if Solzhenitsyn is advocating an authoritarian government for Russia, it seems important to know what kind it will be, and
above all how it will achieve legitimacy and legality. This looks like a
failing of Solzhenitsyn,[1] since the Westerner would want to know more
clearly what he was protesting for, in some detail, before he took the
risks associated with the manifesto 'Live not by lies'. It may seem odd to
the Western mind that Solzhenitsyn intervenes in political affairs while
at the same time rejecting all politics. This attitude is surely not only
ineffective in politics, but also mortally dangerous – or so we might think.

Other criticisms of Solzhenitsyn include the one that he is both
prophetic and apocalyptic, elements common in Russian thought but
less so in Anglo-Saxon countries. Moreover he has a tendency to regard
his own solutions as completely right, and to dismiss other trends, in
particular Marxist reformism; and in this trait of single-mindedness he
resembles Lenin.

There are certain apparent confusions in Solzhenitsyn's thought.
Nationalism and patriotism, even when of the creative and liberal kind,
may not always be compatible with a united world community such as
he advocates. It is not certain that he has fully understood the role of the
individual in history,[2] and some would say that he has misunderstood
his own role. There is no doubt that Solzhenitsyn has failed to understand Western democracies such as the UK and the USA, at least in a
detailed technical sense. Britain and America, with all their uncertain-
ties, moral relativism, pluralism, secularism and the struggle of interest
groups, are alien to him. Yet all this is the very stuff of democracy, and
although apparently weak and confused in comparison with monolithic
totalitarianism, these features are both humane and comprehensible to
those countries in which they are firmly established. Moreover, political
systems incorporating these features are widely understood and still
generally supported, thus solving the problem of political legitimacy
without which no political system can survive. The West, in particular
Britain and America, also has some features of which Solzhenitsyn
should approve: for example, the formation of a genuine public opinion,
and the rule of law.

However, we in the West can learn from Solzhenitsyn's warning. In
our struggles for more democracy, we sometimes overlook a crucial fact:
that politics is not only about forms of government, but also about power
and authority. It is about the conflicts which lead to control over authori-
tative decision-making by those who (temporarily) gain predominance
in those conflicts. An obsession with checks and balances, democratic
forms, proportional representation and paper constitution, important
though these are, can all lead to ineffective government decision-making
and loss of respect for the authority of government, a process which is
ably aided and abetted by irresponsibly free mass media. In the ensuing

chaos a ruthless political faction can sweep away democratic niceties and paper constitutions, or ignore them as though they were chaff. All this is very much in line with Solzhenitsyn's contention that freedom of thought, with its attendant moral relativism and political pluralism, is not an end in itself.

Both the United Kingdom and the United States are suffering profound internal crises. Our societies and political systems, despite long periods of stability, are less secure today than at any time since 1945. Moreover, how long can we in the West ignore the fact that our notions of democracy and government are being rejected all over the world in favour of military regimes or totalitarianism? How long can we go on ignoring the population explosion in the 'Third World' with its attendant poverty and starvation, conditions in which our influence is no longer felt, in which our solutions are no longer effective? Solzhenitsyn is right to warn us about these and other dangers, and many have heard the note of authenticity and seen the red light as a result of his speeches.

As regards the future of Russia, we should not be too hasty in rejecting Solzhenitsyn's ideas. The failure of Soviet Marxism has given rise to a specifically Russian phenomenon: National Bolshevism. All that this philosophy has in common with Marxism is a crudely bowdlerised terminology and some slogans, which are retained because they are necessary for the legitimacy of the existing system and because they convince foreign communists of the existence of common interests. In practice, National Bolshevism may be characterised as follows:

> The Russian people is the noblest in the world; its ancient and its modern history are alike unblemished; Tsarism and Bolshevism are equally irreproachable; the nation neither erred nor sinned either before 1917 or after; we have suffered no loss of moral stature and therefore have no need of self-improvement; there are no nationality problems in relation to the border republics – Lenin's and Stalin's solution was ideal; communism is in fact unthinkable without patriotism; the prospects of Russia/USSR are brilliant; blood alone determines whether one is Russian or non-Russian. As for things spiritual, all trends are admissible. . . . God need not be written with a capital letter, but Government must be.[3]

The similarities between this attitude and German National Socialism of 1933–45 may be more apparent than real, but there is no doubt that such views, linked with still powerful Leninist myths about world revolution, are a danger to world peace. In contrast, Solzhenitsyn's liberal nationalism, Christian principles and emphasis on legality, all of which have a considerable following in Russia and the USSR,[4] represent a countervailing force.

Although Solzhenitsyn's exact proposals for the future of Russia, especially in terms of its future political constitution, are not quite clear, this is not necessarily a weakness. One can hardly blame a former Soviet citizen for being wary of yet another blueprint utopia, yet another ideology, yet another physical revolution. Certainly some of Solzhenitsyn's ideas seem visionary, in particular those ideas relating to economic organisation. But it is too early to dismiss his contention that neither socialism nor capitalism is satisfactory; too early to dismiss as unimportant his emphasis on environmentalism.

In the political sphere, it should be noted that Solzhenitsyn's views have a greater measure of support, in all probability, than the 'Democratic Movement' or the Marxist reformism which is on the wane in the Soviet Union, for all its vogue in the West. It is too early to dismiss the moral and civil disobedience of the manifesto 'Live not by lies' as politically ineffective, just as it is too early to pronounce the constitutional actions of the 'Democratic Movement' or the scholarly rationalisations of Medvedev politically effective. Despite Solzhenitsyn's lack of respect for politics, it should be noted that in his personal life and his public utterances he has demonstrated a sure-footedness which few professional politicians are able to match.

As for Solzhenitsyn's dire and apocalyptic warnings – 'Let history judge'. My own view is that there will be no war with Russia if the West will only show her determination to stand and fight for her freedom. Munich has shown us that there is a measure of safety only in firmness. A crucial strategic factor is the size, quality and deployment of British and American naval forces. It should be said that firmness does not preclude understanding: we should learn Russian in our schools, arrange reciprocal visits, and so on, so that we can understand that great nation and the present dilemmas of her society all the better. I repeat that a firm and understanding attitude can avoid war and promote internal reform.

Finally, as to the success of Solzhenitsyn's overall message, he would, I think, accept the following formulation: he will be as successful, no more and no less, as Berdyayev, Dostoevskii and the *Pochvennichestvo*. It is not yet certain that Leninism will ultimately triumph, or that Solzhenitsyn will fail.

NOTES

1 *Vide*, for example, Thompson Bradley, 'Aleksandr Solzhenitsyn's *Cancer Ward*: the failure of defiant stoicism', in J. Dunlop, R. Haugh and A. Klimoff (eds.), *Aleksandr Solzhenitsyn, Critical Essays and Documentary Materials*, Collier (1972), pp. 295–302.
2 *Vide* Mary McCarthy's fascinating article in *ibid.*, p. 350.
3 *From Under the Rubble*, Collins/Harvill (1975), p. 120.
4 John B. Dunlop, 'The Eleventh Hour', *Frontier* (Summer 1975).

Bibliography

PRIMARY SOURCES

IN RUSSIAN

Books
Aleksandr Solzhenitsyn: Sobranie Sochinenii, Possev (1970), six volumes.
Avgust Chetyrnadtsatovo, Flegon Press (1971).
Arkhipelag GULag, Parts I–VII, YMCA, Paris (1973/74/76).
Bodalsya telyonok s dubom, YMCA, Paris (1975).
Vserossiiskomu Patriarkhu Pimenu–Velikopostnoe Pis'mo, Writers and Scholars International (1972).
Iz pod glyb, YMCA, Paris (1974).
Lenin v Tsyurikhe, YMCA, Paris (1975).
Nobelevskaya Lektsiya, Stenvalley Press (1973).
Pismo Vozhdyam Sovetskovo Soyuza, YMCA, Paris (1974).

Articles
Vestnik Russkovo Khristianskovo Dvizheniya, Nos. 97, 111, 112/113, 114, 115, 116.
Kontinent, No. 1 (1974), No. 2 (1974).
Dve Press-konferentsii (k sborniku 'Iz pod glyb'), YMCA, Paris (1975).
Possev (July/August 1974).
Russkaya Mysl' (17 April 1975).
Novoe Russkoye Slovo (19 July 1975).

IN ENGLISH

Books
August 1914, Bodley Head (1972).
Cancer Ward, Penguin (1968).
The First Circle, Collins/Fontana (1968).
From Under the Rubble, Collins/Harvill (1975).
Gulag Archipelago, Parts I–II, Fontana (1974); Parts III–IV, Collins/Harvill (1975).
Letter to Soviet Leaders, Index on Censorship/Fontana (1974).

The Love-Girl and the Innocent, Penguin Modern Drama (1971).
'Means of transport' and 'In memoriam/A. Tvardovski', *Index*, Vol. 1,
   No. 1 (1972).
Nobel Prize Lecture, Stenvalley Press (1973).
One Day in the Life of Ivan Denisovich, Penguin (1963).
L. Labedz (ed.), *Solzhenitsyn – A Documentary Record*, Penguin (1974).
Stories & Prose Poems, The Bodley Head (1971).

Articles, etc.
The Listener (4 and 25 March 1976).
The Times (2 April 1976).
Radio Liberty Research Bulletin Supplement (3 June 1975).

IN FRENCH

Le Chêne et le Veau, Seuil, Paris (1975).

SECONDARY SOURCES

Books
J. Chaix-Ruy, *Soljenitsyne ou la descente aux enfers*, del Duca, Paris (1970).
J. Dunlop, R. Haugh and A. Klimoff (eds.), *Aleksandr Solzhenitsyn,
   Critical Essays and Documentary Materials*, Collier (1975).
G. Lukács, *Solzhenitsyn*, Merlin Press (1970).
A. Myers, *Solzhenitsyn in Exile*, Pathfinder Press (1974).
G. Nivat and M. Aucouturier (eds.), *Soljenitsyne*, Editions L'Herne,
   Paris (1972).
P. Reddaway (ed.), *Uncensored Russia*, Jonathan Cape (1972).
A. Rothberg, *Alexsander Solzhenitsyn – the major novels*, Cornell (1972).
I. Solovyov and others, *The Last Circle*, Novosti, Moscow (1974).
N. Yakovlev, *Solzhenitsyn's Archipelago of Lies*, Novosti, Moscow (1974).

Articles (Selected)
Robin Blackburn, *New Left Review*, No. 63 (1970).
D. Blagov, *Grani*, Nos. 64, 65 (1967).
Heinrich Böll, *Merkur*, No. 5 (1969).
Canadian Slavonic Papers, Vol. 13, Nos. 2, 3 (1971).
John B. Dunlop, *Frontier*, Vol 18, No. 2. (Summer 1975).
John B. Dunlop, *Survey*, No. 96. (Autumn 1975).
D. Fanger, *Problems of Communism*, (May–June 1972).
Michael Glenny, *Survey*, No. 83 (Spring 1972).
Roman Gul', *Novyi Zhurnal*, No. 104 (1971).
Michael Heller, *Survey*, No. 97. (Winter 1975).

Leopold Labedz, *Survey*, No. 82. (Spring 1972).
Pavel Litvinov, *Index*, Vol. 4, No. 1 (1975).
Roy Medvedev, *Index*, Vol. 3, No. 2 (1974).
D. Powell, *Government and Opposition*, Vol. 7, No. 1 (1971).
Terence des Pres, *Encounter* (September 1971).
Rodis Roujos, *Index*, Vol. 1, No. 1 (1972).
Janis Sapiets (interview), *Encounter* (March 1975).
N. Tarasova, *Ost Europa*, Nos. 10, 11, 12 (1965).

N.B. Michael Nicholson of Lancaster University helped in the preparation of part of this bibliography in 1972.

GENERAL AND SOVIET SOURCES

R. Aris, *The History of Political Thought in Germany*, Cass, London (1965).
I. L. Averbakh, *Ot prestupleniya k trudu* (ed. A. Y. Vyshinskii), Sovetskoe Zakonodatelstvo, Moscow (1936).
N. A. Berdyayev, *The Russian Revolution*, University of Michigan Press, Ann Arbor (1961).
P. V. Bykov, *Siluety dalekogo proshlogo*, Moscow, Leningrad (1930).
E. Burke, *Reflections on the Revolution in France*, Pelican (1968).
R. Conquest, *The Great Terror*, Macmillan (1968).
E. Crankshaw, *Khrushchev's Russia*, Penguin (1959).
A. V. Dicey, *An Introduction to the Study of the Law of the Constitution*, Macmillan (1960.)
F. M. Dostoevskii, *The Devils*, Penguin Classics (1969).
J. B. Dunlop, *The New Russian Revolutionaries*, Nordland (1975).
M. Fainsod, *How Russia is Ruled*, Harvard (1970).
S. E. Finer, *Comparative Government*, Pelican (1970).
M. Florinskii, *Russia: a history and an interpretation*, Macmillan (1953 and 1960).
M. N. Gernet (ed.), *Protiv Smertnoi Kazni*, Moscow (1907).
A. Inkeles and R. Bauer, *The Soviet Citizen*, Harvard University Press, Cambridge, Mass. (1959).
N. V. Krylenko, *Za Pyat Let (1918–22)*, Moscow (1923).
M. Latsis, *Dva Goda borby na Vnutrennom fronte*, Moscow (1920).
V. I. Lenin, *Imperialism, the Highest Stage of Capitalism*, Moscow (1934).
V. I. Lenin, *April Theses*, Moscow (1951).
H. Marcuse, *One-Dimensional Man*, Beacon Press (1964).
R. Medvedev, *Let History Judge*, Macmillan (1972).
R. Medvedev, *On Socialist Democracy*, Macmillan (1975).
B. Nikolaevskii, *Power and the Soviet Elite*, Pall Mall (1966).

E. Oberlander, in *Russia Enters the 20th Century*, ed. Katkov, Methuen (1973).

Plato, *The Republic*.

Protsess Prompartii, Sovetskoe Zakonodatelstvo, Moscow (1931).

L. B. Schapiro, *The Communist Party of the Soviet Union*, Methuen (1975).

L. B. Schapiro, *The Government and Politics of the Soviet Union*, Hutchinson (1970).

L. B. Schapiro, *Rationalism and Nationalism in 19th-Century Russian Political Thought*, Yale University Press (1967).

L. B. Schapiro, *Totalitarianism*, Macmillan (1972).

D. N. Shipov, *Memoirs*, Moscow (1918).

M. Spinka, *Nicholas Berdyayev, Captive of Freedom*, Westminster Press (1950).

J. V. Stalin, *The Foundations of Leninism*, Lawrence & Wishart (1942).

J. V. Stalin, *A Short Course History of the CPSU (b)*, Red Star Press (1973).

P. Stuchka, *Guiding Principles of the Criminal Law*, Moscow (1919).

L. N. Tolstoi, *War and Peace*.

A. Walicki, *The Controversy over Capitalism*, Oxford: Clarendon Press (1969).

Vekhi, Possev (1967): 'Sbornik statei o russkoi intelligentsii'.

A. Y. Vyshinskii, *Ot tyurem k vospitatelnym uchrezdeniyam*, Sovetskoe Zakonodatelstvo, Moscow (1934).

Programma Kommunisticheskoi Partii Sovetskovo Soyuza (1961).
Istoriya Kommunisticheskoi Partii Sovetskovo Soyuza (1959/62/69).

General Index

Index to Fictional Characters